The Upper Room Worshipbook

THE UPPER ROOM

Music and Liturgies
for Spiritual Formation

Compiled and Edited by
ELISE S. ESLINGER

THE UPPER ROOM
Nashville, Tennessee

Book design: Linda Bryant
First printing: April, 1985 (10)
ISBN: 0-8358-0515-8
Printed in the United States of America

CONTENTS

PREFACE

The Upper Room Worshipbook was created to answer a deep-felt need for a single resource which would offer a variety of music and liturgy for contemporary settings of worship, praise, and prayer. With the advent of the Emmaus Movement and the Academy for Spiritual Formation, it became evident that no single resource was available which provided this variety of Protestant-oriented patterns of prayer for the daily office, psalm settings, and multiple styles of traditional, ethnic and contemporary song, and service music for Holy Communion.

With this need apparent and urgent, the Upper Room commissioned the creation of this resource, which seeks to provide plentiful examples of helpful music and basic, useful liturgies. Its flexibility makes the *Worshipbook* suitable for a wide range of uses— for Upper Room programming such as the Walk to Emmaus and the Academy for Spiritual Formation; for small and large groups in local churches; for retreats and conferences; for any group of Christians needing an expanded range of hymns, psalm translations and settings, and daily liturgies.

Careful attention has been given to scriptural content and images helpful for the Christian pilgrim, to inclusive language, and to accessibility for the average worshiping congregation or group. It is hoped that this resource will offer both variety and depth to celebrations and will enhance the spiritual formation of its users in faithful relationship with God and with each other in the spirit of Jesus Christ.

DANNY E. MORRIS
The Academy for Spiritual Formation

ROBERT R. WOOD
The Emmaus Movement

EDITOR'S INTRODUCTION

> Let the word of Christ dwell in you richly, teach and
> admonish one another in all wisdom, and sing psalms
> and hymns and spiritual songs with thankfulness in your
> hearts to God—Colossians 3:16, RSV

To be formed spiritually by the word which would dwell in us richly—how much this depends on our listening to the Spirit, not only within our individual pilgrimages, but in genuine Christian community and through our worship.

Music (hymns, songs, and psalms), by nature a central expression and gift in our life together in the Body of Christ, "flourishes best among those who know how to listen and to love."[1] Christians need frequent rehearsal of listening and loving, provided through patterns of prayer, praise, and service of word and sacrament. We need these "rehearsals for life" in varieties of settings, any day of the week, every season of the year.

Sometimes we forget that God's word may be revealed and embodied in the community not only on Sunday and in festival, but also on every day of the week and in "ordinary" time. Sometimes we forget that God's word is more than *words* (as profound as spoken sound, read, preached, and prayed can be). We even forget that we ourselves are "words" spoken forth by God.[2]

Once more, let us discover in the ordinary rhythms of evening and morning (echoing the dying and rising with Christ) the story of salvation. Once again, let us immerse ourselves in rich images of light and darkness, acknowledging the reality of our own presence or separation from God. In our darkness we remember the profound gift of light which is God-with-us, in Jesus Christ. Let us experience anew the Body which would undergird, daily, our response to the word in the world, for the world.

When we gather, utilizing sound *and* silence as the tongue and ear for our praise, we offer an environment in which God's word can do its teaching, admonishing, forgiving, affirming, challenging work in us and through us. Movement, gesture, and dance may join with attentiveness of the focused body and soul to enhance the receipt of the word in our midst. As we connect the narrative of salvation and its signs of water, bread, and wine with our personal stories, then our "I" is forever transformed to "we."

This *Upper Room Worshipbook* seeks to offer musical resources for ecumenical worship in settings beyond the Sunday service. It was developed most especially with the assistance of leaders and participants in the loving communities of the Academy for Spiritual Formation and the Walk to Emmaus. To them and to the staff of the Upper Room, I am deeply grateful. The *Worshipbook* is intended for use by these and other Upper Room programs. It is also offered to all local churches, ecumenical prayer groups, retreat centers, campus and seminary chapels, conferences, camps, families, and any gatherings of Christians for worship, especially those which occur at times other than Sunday morning.

Included in the *Worshipbook* are patterns of morning, evening, and night prayer, and a service of Holy Communion. For the enrichment of these basic liturgies, I have provided sections of hymns for general use, hymns for morning and evening, and hymns for Holy Communion; of songs; of selected psalmody—the very heart of daily prayer; of responses and rounds; and of selected canticles and service music.

In order to make accessible the riches of musical prayer to many kinds of persons and for many settings, this compilation has been derived from a variety of sources, and in multiple musical styles. Some material is original and previously unpublished. The *Worshipbook* is designed for use in both formal and informal settings, planned or spontaneous happenings. The patterns ("orders") provide secure, tradition-sensitive bases and guidance for contemporary prayer and praise. Simplicity is valued highly. The content has been weighed carefully for theological strength and depth, for fullness and variety of images, for musical accessibility, for potential congregational participation, and for the centrality of scripture. Special attention has been given to the urgent need for inclusive language. Insofar as individual poets and composers would allow, the selections are language inclusive, and the resource is offered in this spirit. Alterations were made where appropriate, and whenever permission was granted. I am especially indebted to the following scholars and musicians for wise liturgical and musical counsel: Dr. Diedra Kriewald, Dr. James Kriewald, Dr. Don Saliers, and Dr. Richard Eslinger.

Each section of the *Worshipbook* is introduced by comments and suggestions intended to enhance practical use of the selections. Those desiring additional material should refer to credit lines for references to specific resources and publishers. We now offer this resource to all those "lost in wonder, love, and praise,"[3] who would seek to know and be known by Jesus Christ; who would seek to find and be found by the God who pursues; who would bring close the world loved so much by the God of *shalom* and touch it with a song, a prayer, and word embodied in acts of compassion and loving service.

ELISE S. ESLINGER
Epiphany Day, 1985

1. Rachael Reeder in *Liturgy 3* (Summer 1983), p. 4.

2. An insight gained from Dr. Robert Mulholland during a lecture to the Academy for Spiritual Formation, May, 1982.

3. Charles Wesley, "Love Divine, All Loves Excelling."

I

HYMNS

Included in this section are both familiar and new hymns for *general use*, for *morning and evening,* and for *Holy Communion*. Certain traditional texts have been matched with new or different tunes. Some texts have been revised for language inclusiveness. Some tunes have been newly arranged. In several cases, multiple texts for the same tune have been provided.

In worship, hymns have long been sung as expression of the people's praise. They have also been utilized as means for biblical and theological reflection. Let the choice of hymns for particular services be appropriate first to the scripture of the day, and also to the time of day, special themes and seasons, and to the setting. Let the performance of the hymn be in appropriately exuberant or reflective manner, experienced in a variety of cultural styles, as called for by the word, and by the life and needs of the community and the world it serves.

Leaders may want to use varieties of congregational "performance" but, overall, should allow the singing to be simple, and not too constrained by demands for "doing," which might obscure meaning or limit free participation. The following are some appropriate ways to provide variety:

1. Sing verses in parts as well as in unison.
2. Alternate verses of men's and women's voices, utilize soloists, or alternate choir and congregation.
3. Add melody or percussive instruments as available and musically appropriate.
4. Read aloud or silently portions of hymn texts for prayer and reflection.
5. Sing both *a capella* and with keyboard or other accompaniment.

In ongoing communities, hymns should be repeated frequently enough that they will be well learned and internalized. One of the useful features of this section is the inclusion of alternate texts with some of the tunes, which by repeated use will become more familiar to the congregation. Such repetition soon allows the hymn to dwell richly, to teach, and to express our thankfulness through God's gift of music.

1 • From All Who Dwell below the Skies

1. From all who dwell be - low the skies, Let
2. E - ter - nal are your mer - cies, Lord, E -
3. Praise God from whom all bless - ings flow, Praise

the Cre - a - tor's praise a - rise: Al - le - lu - ia, al - le -
ter - nal truth at - tends your word: Al - le - lu - ia, al - le -
God, all crea - tures here be - low: Al - le - lu - ia, al - le -

lu - ia. Let the Re - deem - er's name be sung, Through
lu - ia. Your praise shall sound from shore to shore, Till
lu - ia. Praise God a - bove, you heav - 'nly hosts, Praise

Psalm 117
Isaac Watts, alt.
Verse 3, Thomas Ken, alt.

LASST UNS ERFREUEN
Arr. Sister Theophane Hytrek

ev - 'ry land, by ev - 'ry tongue. Al - le - lu - ia, al - le -
suns shall rise and set no more. Al - le - lu - ia, al - le -
Fath - er, Son and Ho - ly Ghost. Al - le - lu - ia, al - le -

lu - ia, Al - le - lu - ia, al - le - lu - ia, al - le - lu - ia.
lu - ia, Al - le - lu - ia, al - le - lu - ia, al - le - lu - ia.
lu - ia, Al - le - lu - ia, al - le - lu - ia, al - le - lu - ia.

1A • Creating God, Your Fingers Trace

Alternate Text

1. Creating God, your fingers trace The bold designs of farthest space;
   Alleluia, alleluia.
   Let sun and moon and stars and light And what lies hidden praise your might.
   Alleluia, alleluia, alleluia, alleluia, alleluia.

2. Sustaining God, your hands uphold Earth's myst'ries known or yet untold;
   Alleluia, alleluia.
   Let waters fragile blend with air, Enabling life, proclaim our care.
   Alleluia, alleluia, alleluia, alleluia, alleluia.

3. Redeeming God, your arms embrace All now oppressed for creed or race;
   Alleluia, alleluia.
   Let peace descending as the dove Make known on earth your healing love.
   Alleluia, alleluia, alleluia, alleluia, alleluia.

4. Indwelling God, your gospel claims One fam'ly with a billion names;
   Alleluia, alleluia.
   Let every life be touched by grace Until we praise you face to face.
   Alleluia, alleluia, alleluia, alleluia, alleluia.

Jeffery Rowthorn, adapt.

2 • Praise Be to God, the Almighty

1. Praise be to God, the Al - might - y, who rules all cre - a - tion! O my soul, wor - ship the well - spring of health and sal - va - tion! Let all who hear Now to God's tem - ple draw near, Join - ing in glad ad - o - ra - tion!

2. Praise be to God, who o'er all things is won - drous - ly reign - ing, Bring - ing new life, in great mer - cy re - deem - ing, sus - tain - ing. Pon - der a - new What the Al - might - y can do; Pon - der God's gra - cious or - dain - ing.

3. Praise be to God, who works jus - tice, who ends all op - press - ing! God's name most ho - ly let Is - ra - el al - ways be bless - ing! Rise up on wings! Heal - ing and whole - ness God brings! Al - ways God's deeds be con - fess - ing!

4. Praise be to God! O for - get not God's man - i - fold gra - ces! All that has life and breath, one song of grat - i - tude rais - es! Let the a - men Sound from God's peo - ple a - gain. Glad - ly for - ev - er sing prais - es!

Psalm 103
Joachim Neander
Trans. by Catherine Winkworth *et al.*
New words by Ruth Duck

LOBE DEN HERREN

New words, Ruth Duck, 1980. Reprinted by her permission from *Everflowing Streams: Songs for Worship* (Pilgrim Press, 1981). Setting from Orgelchoralbuch Wurttemberg Ⓒ Gesangbuchverlag der Evangelischen Landeskirche Wurttemberg, Stuttgart. Used by permission.

3 • Joyful, Joyful, We Adore Thee

1. Joy - ful, joy - ful, we a - dore thee, God of glo - ry, God of love;
2. All thy works with joy sur-round thee, Earth and heav'n re - flect thy rays,
3. Thou art giv - ing and for - giv - ing, Ev - er bless - ing, ev - er blest,
4. Mor - tals, join the might - y cho - rus; Stars of morn - ing, take your part;

Hearts un - fold like flowers be - fore thee, Open - ing to the sun a - bove.
Stars and an - gels sing a - round thee, Cen - ter of un - bro - ken praise.
Well - spring of the joy of liv - ing, O - cean depth of hap - py rest!
Love di - vine is reign - ing o'er us, Bind - ing those of ten - der heart;

Melt the clouds of sin and sad - ness, Drive the dark of doubt a - way;
Field and for - est, vale and moun-tain, Flow - ery mead-ow, flash - ing sea,
God, Cre - a - tor, Christ, Re - deem - er, All who live in love are thine;
Ev - er sing - ing, mov - ing on - ward, Lov - ing in the midst of strife,

Giv - er of im - mor - tal glad - ness, Fill us with the light of day.
Chant-ing bird and flow - ing foun-tain, Call us to re - joice in thee.
Teach us how to love each oth - er, Lift us to the joy di - vine.
Joy - ful mu - sic leads us sun-ward In the tri - umph song of life.

Henry Van Dyke, alt.

HYMN TO JOY
Arr. from Ludwig van Beethoven
by Edward Hodges

Henry Van Dyke, "Joyful, Joyful We Adore Thee" in THE POEMS OF HENRY VAN DYKE. Courtesy of Charles Scribner's Sons. Alteration of words printed with permission of the Ecumenical Women's Center, 5253 N. Kenmore, Chicago, IL 60640, © 1974.

4 • Praise, My Soul, the God of Heaven

1. Praise, my soul, the God of heav - en, Glad of heart your car - ols raise; Ran - somed, healed, re - stored, for - giv - en, Who, like me, should sing God's praise? Al - le - lu - ia! Al - le - lu - ia! Praise the Mak - er all your days!
2. Praise God for the grace and fa - vor Shown our fore - bears in dis - tress; God is still the same for - ev - er, Slow to chide, and swift to bless. Al - le - lu - ia! Al - le - lu - ia! Sing our Mak - er's faith - ful - ness!
3. Like a lov - ing par - ent car - ing, God knows well our fee - ble frame; Glad - ly all our bur - dens bear - ing, Still to count - less years the same. Al - le - lu - ia! Al - le - lu - ia! All with - in me, praise God's name!
4. An - gels teach us ad - o - ra - tion, You be - hold God face to face; Sun and moon and all cre - a - tion, Dwell - ers all in time and space, Al - le - lu - ia! Al - le - lu - ia! Praise with us the God of grace!

Psalm 103
Henry F. Lyte,
Adapt. Ecumenical Women's Center

LAUDA ANIMA
John Goss

4A • God, Whose Love Is Reigning O'er Us

Alternate Text

1. God, whose love is reigning o'er us, Source of all, the ending true;
   Hear the universal chorus Raised in joyful praise to you:
   Alleluia, alleluia, Worship ancient, worship new.

2. Word of God from nature bringing Springtime green and autumn gold;
   Mountain streams like children singing, Ocean waves like thunder bold:
   Alleluia, alleluia, As creation's tale is told.

3. Yahweh, God of ancient glory, Choosing man and woman, too;
   Abram's faith and Sarah's story Formed a people bound to you:
   Alleluia, alleluia, To your cov'nant keep us true.

4. Cov'nant, new again in Jesus, Star-child born to set us free;
   Sent to heal us, sent to teach us How love's children we might be:
   Alleluia, alleluia, Risen Christ, our Savior He!

5. Lift we then our human voices, In the songs that faith would bring;
   Live we then in human choices Lives that like our music, sing:
   Alleluia, alleluia, Joined in love our praises ring!

William Boyd Grove

Words used by permission of Bishop William Boyd Grove.

5 • In God's Image*

(God, Who Spins the Whirling Planets)

1. God, who spins the whirl-ing plan-ets, Fills the seas and spreads the plain,
2. You have called us to be faith-ful In our life and min-is-try.
3. God, your word is still cre-a-ting, Call-ing us to life made new.

Molds the moun-tains, fash-ions blos-soms, Calls forth sun-shine, wind, and rain:
We re-spond in grate-ful wor-ship, Joined in one com-mu-ni-ty.
Now re-veal to us fresh vis-tas Where there's work to dare and do.

We, cre-a-ted in your im-age, Would a true re-flec-tion be
When we blur your gra-cious im-age, Fo-cus us and make us whole.
Keep us clear of all dis-tor-tion. Pol-ish us, with lov-ing care.

Of your jus-tice, grace, and mer-cy, And the truth that makes us free.
Healed and strength-ened, as your peo-ple, We move on-ward toward your goal.
Thus new crea-tures in your im-age, We'll pro-claim Christ ev-ery-where.

*May be sung to tune HOLY MANNA, No. 5 A.
Jane Parker Huber

AUSTRIAN HYMN
Franz Joseph Haydn

5A • God, Who Stretched the Spangled Heavens*

Not too fast
UNISON

1. God, who stretched the span-gled heav - ens, in - fi - nite in time and place,
2. Proud-ly rise our mod-ern cit - ies, state - ly build-ings, row by row;
3. We have ven-tured worlds un dreamed of since the child-hood of our race.
4. As each far ho - ri - zon beck - ons, may it chal-lenge us a - new.

Flung the suns in burn - ing ra - diance through the si - lent fields of space;
Yet their win-dows, blank, un - feel - ing, stare on can-yoned streets be-low,
Known the ec - sta - sy of wing-ing through trav - eled realms of space;
Chil - dren of cre - a - tive pur - pose, serv - ing oth - ers, hon - 'ring you.

We, your chil - dren in your like-ness share in - ven - tive powers with you;
Where the lone - ly drift un - no - ticed in the ci - ty's ebb and flow,
Probed the se - crets of the at - om, yield-ing un - i - mag - ined power,
May our dreams prove rich with prom-ise, each en - deav - or well be - gun:

Great cre - a - tor, still cre - a - ting, Show us what we yet may do.
Lost to pur - pose and to mean-ing, scarce - ly car - ing where they go.
Fa - cing us with life's de - struc - tion or our most tri - um-phant hour.
Great cre - a - tor, give us guid - ance till our goals and yours are one.

*May be sung to tune AUSTRIAN HYMN, No. 5.

Catherine Cameron

HOLY MANNA
William Moore
Arr. Elise S. Eslinger

6 • God, Whose Almighty Word

1. God, whose al - might - y word / Cha - os and
2. Lord, who once came to bring, / On your re -
3. Spir - it of truth and love, / Life - giv - ing,
4. Ho - ly and bless - ed three, / Glo - ri - ous

dark - ness heard / And took their flight:
deem - ing wing, / Heal - ing and sight,
ho - ly dove, / Speed forth your flight;
Trin - i - ty, / Wis - dom, love, might!

Hear us, we hum - bly pray, / And where the Gos - pel day
Health to the sick in mind, / Sight to the in - ly blind:
Move on the wa - ter's face / Bear - ing the lamp of grace,
Bound - less as o - cean's tide, / Roll - ing in full - est pride,

Sheds not its glo - rious ray,
Oh, now to hu - man - kind, / Let there be light!
And in earth's dark - est place,
Through the earth, far and wide,

John Marriott, alt.

ITALIAN HYMN
Felice de Giardini

7 • Easter People, Raise Your Voices

1. Eas - ter peo - ple, raise your voic - es, Sounds of heav'n in
2. Fear of death can no more stop us, From our press - ing
3. Ev - 'ry day to us is Eas - ter, With its Res - ur -

earth should ring. Christ has brought us heav - en's choic - es
here be - low. For our Lord has now em - pow'red us
rec - tion song. When in trou - ble move the fast - er

Heav'n - ly mu - sic, let it ring. Al - le - lu - ia!
To tri - umph o - ver ev - 'ry foe. Al - le - lu - ia!
To our God who rights the wrong. Al - le - lu - ia!

Al - le - lu - ia! Eas - ter peo - ple, let us sing.
Al - le - lu - ia! On to vic - t'ry row we go.
Al - le - lu - ia! See the pow'r of heav'n - ly throngs.

William M. James

REGENT SQUARE
Henry Smart

7A • For the Healing of the Nations

Alternate Text

1. For the healing of the nations, Lord, we pray with one accord;
   For a just and equal sharing Of the things that earth affords.
   To a life of love in action Help us rise and pledge our word.

2. You, Creator God, have written Your great name on humankind;
   For our growing in Your likeness Bring the life of Christ to mind;
   That by our response and service Earth its destiny may find.

Fred Kaan

8 • A Prayer for Healing
(To You, O Lord)

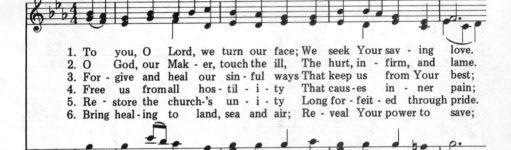

1. To you, O Lord, we turn our face; We seek Your sav - ing love.
2. O God, our Mak - er, touch the ill, The hurt, in - firm, and lame.
3. For - give and heal our sin - ful ways That keep us from Your best;
4. Free us from all hos - til - i - ty That caus - es in - ner pain;
5. Re - store the church's un - i - ty Long for - feit - ed through pride.
6. Bring heal - ing to land, sea and air; Re - veal Your power to save;

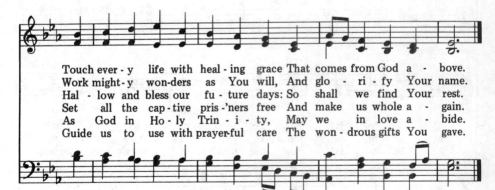

Touch ev - er - y life with heal - ing grace That comes from God a - bove.
Work might - y won - ders as You will, And glo - ri - fy Your name.
Hal - low and bless our fu - ture days: So shall we find Your rest.
Set all the cap - tive pris - 'ners free And make us whole a - gain.
As God in Ho - ly Trin - i - ty, May we in love a - bide.
Guide us to use with prayer - ful care The won - drous gifts You gave.

Kenneth Cain Kinghorn

AQUEDUCT
Kenneth Cain Kinghorn
Alternate tune: AMAZING GRACE, No. 17

9 • Give Us, O God, the Grace to See

1. Give us, O God, the grace to see Your
2. Give us, O God, the grace to hear Your
3. Give us, O God, the grace to feel Your
4. Give us, O God, the grace to be Con -

smile with - in the morn - ing light; Your
Word when mar - ble turns to clay; Your
breath up - on the winds of change; Your
vinced when mir - a - cles are rare; Your

sig - na - ture up - on the sea; Your
voice when thun - der clouds ap - pear; Your
kiss in sac - ra - ments that heal; Your
truth when stars turn eb - o - ny; Your

shad - ow in the black - est night.
an - swer when the moun - tains sway.
hand in what the years ar - range.
saints till earth has no de - spair.

Roger Kronmann

JORDAN
Jordon Cho-tung Tang
Alternate tune: TALLIS' CANON, No. 21

10 • Eternal God, in Whom We Live and Move

1. E - ter - nal God in whom we live and move,
2. Bap - tize your peo - ple with your Spir - it, Lord;
3. Spir - it of God, be - stow your grace, we pray;
4. Lift up your Church, Lord; give us eyes to see

Who from our birth has kept us in your love.
Re - new with - in us Christ, the liv - ing Word.
In - spire our thoughts, Lord, all we do and say.
All that our Mas - ter now would have her be.

Who would af - firm your grace in this high hour,
We have a vis - ion of your king - dom near;
Make strong our lives, O keep us in your Way.
Hold fast our trust and make our wit - ness true.

And rest our lives in your re - deem - ing power.
Judge us and guide us, make your pre - cepts clear.
Lead us, your pil - grims, through each night and day.
We live to serve you; make our world a - new.

Chester E. Custer

MORECAMBE
Frederick C. Atkinson

11 • Christ Is the Truth, the Way

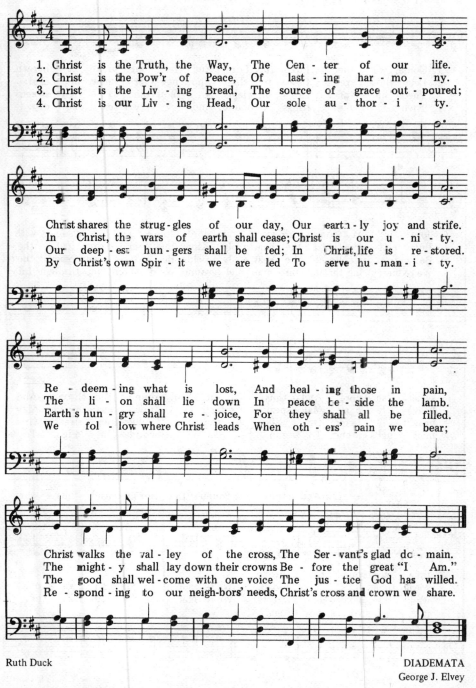

1. Christ is the Truth, the Way, The Cen - ter of our life.
2. Christ is the Pow'r of Peace, Of last - ing har - mo - ny.
3. Christ is the Liv - ing Bread, The source of grace out - poured;
4. Christ is our Liv - ing Head, Our sole au - thor - i - ty.

Christ shares the strug - gles of our day, Our earth - ly joy and strife.
In Christ, the wars of earth shall cease; Christ is our u - ni - ty.
Our deep - est hun - gers shall be fed; In Christ, life is re - stored.
By Christ's own Spir - it we are led To serve hu - man - i - ty.

Re - deem - ing what is lost, And heal - ing those in pain,
The li - on shall lie down In peace be - side the lamb.
Earth's hun - gry shall re - joice, For they shall all be filled.
We fol - low where Christ leads When oth - ers' pain we bear;

Christ walks the val - ley of the cross, The Ser - vant's glad do - main.
The might - y shall lay down their crowns Be - fore the great "I Am."
The good shall wel - come with one voice The jus - tice God has willed.
Re - spond - ing to our neigh-bors' needs, Christ's cross and crown we share.

Ruth Duck

DIADEMATA
George J. Elvey

Words by Ruth Duck © 1981. Reprinted by her permission from *Everflowing Streams: Songs for Worship* (Pilgrim Press, 1981).

12 • We're Marching to Zion
(Come, We That Love the Lord)

1. Come, we that love the Lord, And let our joys be known.
2. Let those re - fuse to sing Who nev - er knew our God:
3. The hill of Zi - on yields A thou - sand sa - cred sweets
4. Then let our songs a - bound, And ev - 'ry tear be dry:

Join in a song with sweet ac - cord, Join in a song with
But chil - dren of the heav'n - ly King, But chil - dren of the
Be - fore we reach the heav'n - ly fields, Be - fore we reach the
We're march - ing through Im - man - uel's ground, We're march - ing through Im -

sweet ac - cord, And thus sur - round the throne, And
heav'n - ly King, May speak their joys a - broad, May
heav'n - ly fields, Or walk the gold - en streets, Or
man - uel's ground. To fair - er worlds on high, To

1. And thus sur - round the throne, And thus sur -

Refrain

thus sur - round the throne.
speak their joys a - broad. We're march - ing to Zi - on,
walk the gold - en streets. We're march - ing on to Zi - on,
fair - er worlds on high.

round the throne.

Isaac Watts
Refrain by Robert Lowry

MARCHING TO ZION
Robert Lowry

Beau - ti - ful, beau - ti - ful Zi - on; We're march - ing up - ward to

Zi - on,
Zi - on, Zi - on, The beau - ti - ful cit - y of God.

13 • The Care the Eagle Gives Her Young

1. The care the ea - gle gives her young, Safe in her lof - ty nest,
2. As when the time to ven - ture comes, She stirs them out to flight,
3. And if we flut - ter help - less - ly, As fledg - ling ea - gles fall,

Is like the ten - der love of God For us made man - i - fest.
So we are pressed to bold - ly try To strive for dar - ing height.
Be - neath us lift God's might - y wings To bear us one and all.

Deuteronomy 32:11
R. Deane Postlethwaite (1925-1980)

CAMPMEETING

14 • The Church's One Foundation

Unison

1. The Church's one foun-da-tion Is Je-sus Christ our Lord;
2. Called forth from ev-'ry na-tion, Yet one o'er all the earth;
3. Though with a scorn-ful won-der The world sees us op-pressed,

We are his new cre-a-tion By wa-ter and the Word;
Our char-ter of sal-va-tion: One Lord, one faith, one birth.
By schi-sms rent a-sun-der, By her-e-sies dis-tressed,

From heav'n he came and sought us That we might ev-er be
One ho-ly Name pro-fes-sing And at one ta-ble fed,
Yet saints their watch are keep-ing; Their cry goes up, "How long?"

His liv-ing ser-vant peo-ple, By his own death set free.
To one hope al-ways pres-sing, By Christ's own spir-it led.
But soon the night of weep-ing Shall be the morn of song.

4. 'Mid toil and tribulation,
And tumult of our war,
We wait the consummation
Of peace forevermore;
Till with the vision glorious
Our longing eyes are blest,
And the great Church victorious
Shall be the Church at rest.

5. We now on earth have union
With God, the Three in One,
And share through faith communion
With those whose rest is won.
Oh, happy ones, and holy!
Lord, give us grace that we
Like them, the meek and lowly,
On high may dwell with thee.

Samuel J. Stone
Adapt. Laurence Hull Stookey

WEDLOCK
Harm. Austin C. Lovelace
Alternative tune: AURELIA

15 • Holy Spirit, Truth Divine

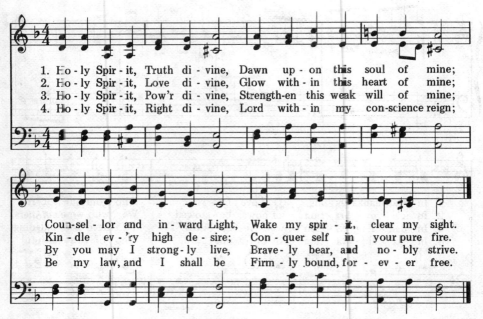

1. Ho - ly Spir - it, Truth di - vine, Dawn up - on this soul of mine;
2. Ho - ly Spir - it, Love di - vine, Glow with - in this heart of mine;
3. Ho - ly Spir - it, Pow'r di - vine, Strength-en this weak will of mine;
4. Ho - ly Spir - it, Right di - vine, Lord with - in my con-science reign;

Coun - sel - lor and in - ward Light, Wake my spir - it, clear my sight.
Kin - dle ev - 'ry high de - sire; Con - quer self in your pure fire.
By you may I strong - ly live, Brave - ly bear, and no - bly strive.
Be my law, and I shall be Firm - ly bound, for - ev - er free.

5. Holy Spirit, Peace divine, Still this restless heart of mine;
   Speak to calm this tossing sea, Stayed in your tranquility.

6. Holy Spirit, Joy divine, Gladden now this heart of mine;
   In the desert ways I sing, "Spring, O Well, forever spring."

Samuel Longfellow

AUS DER TIEFE
Attr. Martin Herbst

15A • Take My Life, and Let It Be Consecrated

Alternate Text

1. Take my life, and let it be Consecrated, Lord, to thee.
   Take my moments and my days; Let them flow in ceaseless praise.

2. Take my hands, and let them move At the impulse of thy love.
   Take my feet, and let them be Swift and beautiful for thee.

3. Take my voice, and let me sing Always, only, for my King.
   Take my lips, and let them be Filled with messages from thee.

4. Take my silver and my gold; Not a mite would I withhold.
   Take my intellect and use Ev'ry pow'r as thou shalt choose.

5. Take my will and make it thine; It shall be no longer mine.
   Take my heart, it is thine own; It shall be thy royal throne.

6. Take my love; my Lord, I pour At thy feet its treasure-store.
   Take myself, and I will be Ever, only, all for thee.

Frances R. Havergal

16 • In Great Thanksgiving

1. In great thanks-giv - ing, O Love Di - vine, Who from our sor - row
2. In cel - e - bra - tion of power be - stowed, We who were sin - ners
3. In ded - i - ca - tion we give our lives To heed your bid - ding
4. In ex - al - ta - tion of Christ our Lord, Who for the faith-ful

re - deemed us all, Cleansed of re - gret - ting,
are fol - l'wers bold, For - giv - ing en' - mies
to seek the lost, To all the hun - gry
true life en - sured, We laud him Sav - ior,

re - lieved of fear, We come re - joic - ing for new life here.
we sing your praise, With ju - bi - la - tion, love's ban-ner raise.
bring food for feasts, To fear-bound peo-ple strength for life's tests.
we teach his way Of peace with jus-tice, hope for to - day.

Melchizedek M. Solis

MALATE
Mutya Lopez Solis

Words and music by Melchizedek and Mutya Solis © 1983 in *Hymns from the Four Winds*. Used by permission.

17 • Lord Jesus, As We Turn from Sin

No* too fast
UNISON

1. Lord Je - sus, as we turn from sin With strength and hope re - stored, Re - ceive the hom - age that we bring To you, our ris - en Lord.
2. We call on you whose liv - ing word Has made the Fath - er known, O Shep - herd, we have wan - dered far. Find us and lead us home.
3. Your glance at Pe - ter helped him know The love he had de - nied, Now gaze on us and heal us, Lord, Of sel - fish - ness and pride.
4. Reach out and touch with heal - ing pow'r The wounds we have re - ceived, That in for - give - ness we may love And may no long - er grieve.
5. Then stay with us when eve - ning comes And dark - ness makes us blind, O stay un - til the light of dawn May fill both heart and mind.

Ralph Wright

AMAZING GRACE
Arr. Elise S. Eslinger

18 • Father, We Praise You

1. Fa - ther, we praise you, now the night is o - ver, Ac - tive and
2. Mon - arch of all things, fit us for your man - sions; Ban - ish our
3. All - ho - ly Fa - ther, Son, and e - qual Spir - it, Trin - i - ty

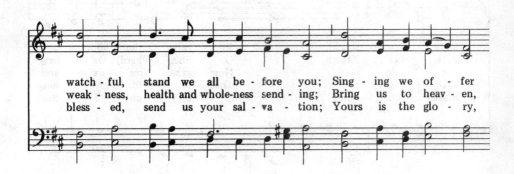

watch - ful, stand we all be - fore you; Sing - ing we of - fer
weak - ness, health and whole-ness send - ing; Bring us to heav - en,
bless - ed, send us your sal - va - tion; Yours is the glo - ry,

prayer and med - i - ta - tion; Thus we a - dore you.
where your Saints u - nit - ed Joy with - out end - ing.
gleam - ing and re - sound - ing Through all cre - a - tion.

Attr. Gregory I
Trans. Percy Dearmer (1867-1936) altd.

CHRISTE SANCTORUM
Antiphoner

18A • Father Most Holy

Alternate Text

1. Father most holy, merciful and tender;
   Jesus our Savior, with the Father reigning;
   Spirit all kindly, Advocate, Defender,
   Light never waning;

2. Trinity sacred, Unity unshaken;
   Deity perfect, giving and forgiving,
   Light of the Angels, Life of the forsaken,
   Hope of all living;

3. Maker of all things, all thy creatures praise thee:
   Lo, all things serve thee through thy whole creation:
   Hear us, Almighty, hear us as we raise thee
   Heart's adoration.

4. To the all-ruling triune God be glory;
   Highest and greatest, help thou our endeavor,
   We too would praise thee, giving honor worthy,
   Now and forever.

Latin hymn
Trans. Percy Dearmer (1867-1936) altd.

From the *English Hymnal* by permission of Oxford University Press.

19 • Arise, Your Light Has Come

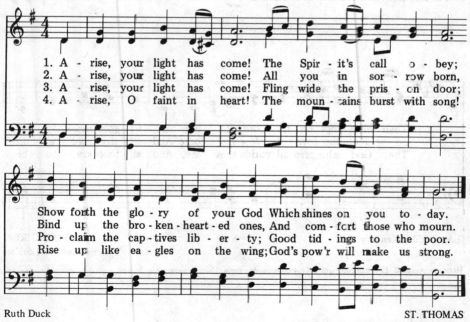

1. A - rise, your light has come! The Spir - it's call o - bey;
2. A - rise, your light has come! All you in sor - row born,
3. A - rise, your light has come! Fling wide the pris - on door;
4. A - rise, O faint in heart! The moun - tains burst with song!

Show forth the glo - ry of your God Which shines on you to - day.
Bind up the bro - ken - heart - ed ones, And com - fort those who mourn.
Pro - claim the cap - tives lib - er - ty; Good tid - ings to the poor.
Rise up like ea - gles on the wing; God's pow'r will make us strong.

Ruth Duck

ST. THOMAS
Williams' *New Universal Psalmodist*, 1770

20 • Awake, Awake to Love and Work

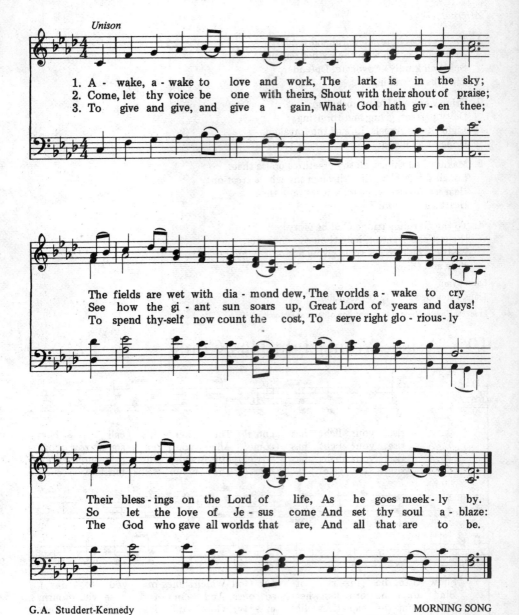

Unison

1. A - wake, a - wake to love and work, The lark is in the sky;
2. Come, let thy voice be one with theirs, Shout with their shout of praise;
3. To give and give, and give a - gain, What God hath giv - en thee;

The fields are wet with dia - mond dew, The worlds a - wake to cry
See how the gi - ant sun soars up, Great Lord of years and days!
To spend thy-self now count the cost, To serve right glo - rious - ly

Their bless - ings on the Lord of life, As he goes meek - ly by.
So let the love of Je - sus come And set thy soul a - blaze:
The God who gave all worlds that are, And all that are to be.

G. A. Studdert-Kennedy

MORNING SONG
Harm. Austin C. Lovelace

21 • New Every Morning

1. New ev-ery morn-ing is the love Our wak-ening and up-ris-ing prove; Through sleep and dark-ness safe-ly brought, Re-stored to life and power and thought.

2. New mer-cies, each re-turn-ing day, Hov-er a-round us while we pray; New per-ils past, new sins for-given, New thoughts of God, new hopes of heaven.

3. The triv-ial round, the com-mon task, Will fur-nish all we ought to ask, If on our dai-ly course our mind Be set to hal-low all we find.

4. On-ly, O Lord, in thy dear love Fit us for per-fect rest a-bove; And help us, this and ev-ery day, To live more near-ly as we pray.

*May be sung as canon.
**Guitar chords for use when not singing as canon.

John Keble

TALLIS' CANON

21A • O Splendor of God's Glory Bright

Alternate Text

1. O Splendor of God's glory bright,
   From Light eternal bringing light,
   O Light of life, light's living Spring,
   True Day, all days illumining:

2. Come, very Sun of heaven's love,
   In lasting radiance from above,
   And pour the Holy Spirit's ray
   On all we think or do today.

3. Confirm our will to do the right,
   And keep our hearts from envy's blight;
   Let faith her eager fires renew,
   And hate the false, and love the true.

4. O joyful be the passing day
   With thoughts as clear as morning's ray,
   With faith like noontide shining bright,
   Our souls unshadowed by the night.

5. Dawn's glory gilds the earth and skies;
   Let him, our perfect Morn, arise,
   The Word in God Creator one,
   The Father imaged in the Son.

Ambrose of Milan, alt.

21B • God of the Morning and of Night

Alternate Text

1. God of the morning and of night,
   We thank you for your gifts of light;
   As in the dawn the shadows fly,
   We seem to find you now more nigh.

2. Fresh hopes have wakened in the heart,
   Fresh force to do our daily part;
   In peaceful sleep our strength restore,
   Throughout the day to serve you more.

3. O Lord of light, your love alone
   Can make our human hearts your own;
   Be ever with us, Lord, that we
   Your blessed face one day may see.

4. Praise God, our maker and our friend;
   Praise God through time, till time shall end;
   Till psalm and song Christ's name adore,
   Through heav'ns great day of evermore.

Francis Turner Palgrave, alt.

21C • All Praise to You

Alternate Text

1. All praise to you, O God, this night,
   For all the blessings of the light,
   Keep us, we pray, O King of Kings,
   Beneath your own almighty wings.

2. Forgive us, Lord, through Christ your Son,
   Whatever wrong this day we've done;
   Your peace give to the world, O Lord,
   That all might live in one accord.

3. Enlighten us, O blessed Light,
   And give us rest throughout this night.
   O strengthen us, that for your sake,
   We all may serve you when we wake.

Thomas Ken, alt.

21D • Phos Hileron
(O Radiant Light)

Alternate Text

1. O radiant light of Light, out-poured
   Eternal brightness, blest, adored,
   From God the Father, holy Lord.
   Alleluia, alleluia.

2. The darkness falls, but here we see
   The evening lights; on bended knee
   We praise you, holy Trinity.
   Alleluia, alleluia.

3. Life giving Son of God, your ways
   Lighten all nations, thus we raise
   To you, Most Worthy, songs of praise.
   Alleluia, alleluia.

Greek Hymn
Adapt. Arlo D. Duba, 1983. Used by permission.

21E • As Pilgrims on Our Way
(Can We, As Pilgrims)

Alternate Text

1. Can we, as pilgrims on our way,
   Confess our faith in God today
   As we recall from journeys past
   The signs that held our purpose fast?

2. When we have used the gift of prayer
   We've known, in quiet, God was there.
   With others we have joined in praise
   And felt, with joy, our spirits blaze.

3. When we have seen compassion shown,
   We have believed it was God's own.
   Creative moments, bright and rare,
   Made new beginnings everywhere.

4. Through scripture understanding grew;
   God's story was our story too.
   Glory we saw through other eyes.
   Examples came in splendid lives.

5. We will, as pilgrims on our way,
   Confess our faith in God today;
   For we recall from journeys past
   The signs that held our purpose fast.

R. Deane Postlethwaite (1925-80)

Used by permission of Marjean Postlethwaite.

21F • O Holy One

1. O Holy One in whom we live,
   In whom we are, in whom we move,
   All glory, laud and praise receive
   For your creating, steadfast love.

2. Come, Holy Spirit, and inspire,
   Enlighten with celestial fire;
   Impart your grace, our souls unite,
   Renew the dullness of our sight.

3. All praise to God, the Three-in-One,
   All glory to our Christ, the Son,
   And to the Spirit, Holy Power,
   We give our hearts in this glad hour.

4. Alleluia, Alleluia, Alleluia, Alleluia,
   Alleluia, Alleluia, Alleluia, Amen, Amen.

Varied sources, adapt.

Elise S. Eslinger

22 • O Christ, You Are the Light and Day

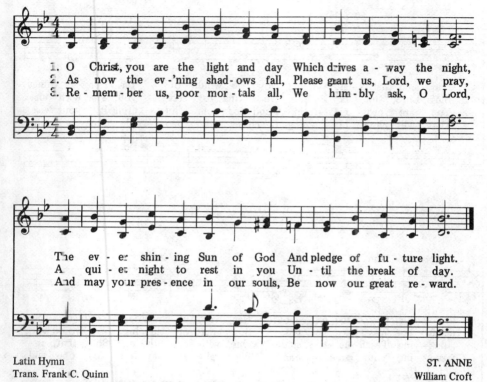

1. O Christ, you are the light and day Which drives a - way the night,
2. As now the ev -'ning shad - ows fall, Please grant us, Lord, we pray,
3. Re - mem - ber us, poor mor - tals all, We hum - bly ask, O Lord,

The ev - er shin - ing Sun of God And pledge of fu - ture light.
A qui - et night to rest in you Un - til the break of day.
And may your pres - ence in our souls, Be now our great re - ward.

Latin Hymn
Trans. Frank C. Quinn

ST. ANNE
William Croft

Trans. Frank C Quinn, O.P. Copyright © 1981 St. Dominic Priory.

22A • Hymn to the Trinity
(Creator God, Creating Still)

Alternate Text

1. Creator God, creating still,
   By will and word and deed.
   Create a new humanity
   To meet the present need.

2. Redeemer God, redeeming still,
   With overflowing grace,
   Pour out your love on us, through us,
   Make this a holy place

3. Sustainer God, sustaining still,
   With strength for every day,
   Empower us now to do your will,
   Correct us when we stray.

4. Great Trinity for this new day,
   We need your presence still.
   Create, redeem, sustain us now
   To do your work and will.

Jane Parker Huber

23 • Praise and Thanksgiving

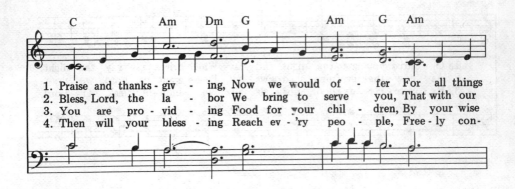

1. Praise and thanks-giv - ing, Now we would of - fer For all things
2. Bless, Lord, the la - bor We bring to serve you, That with our
3. You are pro-vid - ing Food for your chil - dren, By your wise
4. Then will your bless - ing Reach ev-'ry peo - ple, Free-ly con-

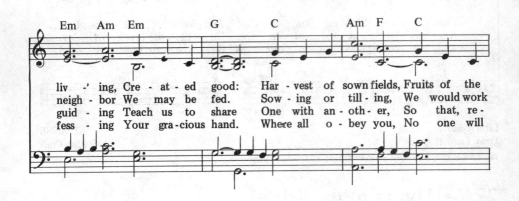

liv-'ing, Cre-at-ed good: Har - vest of sown fields, Fruits of the
neigh - bor We may be fed. Sow - ing or till - ing, We would work
guid - ing Teach us to share One with an-oth - er, So that, re-
fess - ing Your gra-cious hand. Where all o - bey you, No one will

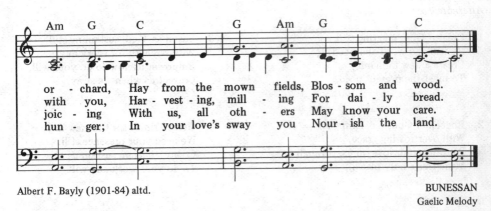

or - chard, Hay from the mown fields, Blos - som and wood.
with you, Har - vest - ing, mill - ing For dai - ly bread.
joic - ing With us, all oth - ers May know your care.
hun - ger; In your love's sway you Nour-ish the land.

Albert F. Bayly (1901-84) altd.

BUNESSAN
Gaelic Melody

23A • Morning Has Broken

Alternate Text

1. Morning has broken Like the first morning,
   Blackbird has spoken Like the first bird.
   Praise for the singing! Praise for the morning!
   Praise for them, springing Fresh from the Word!

2. Sweet the rain's new fall Sunlit from heaven,
   Like the first dewfall On the first grass.
   Praise for the sweetness Of the wet garden,
   Sprung in completeness Where His feet pass.

3. Mine is the sunlight! Mine is the morning
   Born of the one light Eden saw play!
   Praise with elation, Praise every morning,
   God's recreation of the new day!

Eleanor Farjeon

Words by Eleanor Farjeon from THE CHILDREN'S BELLS, published by Oxford University Press. Used by permission of David Higham Associates Ltd.

23B • Water Has Held Us

Alternate Text

1. Water has held us, Moved by creation.
   Out of dark chaos, Broke forth the light.
   Up from the deluge, Showing God's promise,
   Has come a rainbow. Gladdening sight.

2. Water has saved us, As the sea parted
   For Israel's children, Walled on each side.
   This love has led us, helped us in trouble,
   On far horizon, God's cloud our guide.

3. Water has cleansed us, Bathed with forgiveness,
   Has, with clear blessing, Washed sin away.
   Jordan's strong currents God's Son announcing,
   Made a beginning, baptismal day.

4. Water has touched us, fresh on our foreheads,
   Showing an inward, spiritual grace.
   Into God's family we have been welcomed,
   As sons and daughters, we take our place.

R. Deane Postlethwaite (1925-1980)

Words used by permission of Marjean Postlethwaite.

24 • Lord of All Hopefulness

1. Lord of all hope-ful-ness, Lord of all joy, Whose trust, ev-er child-like, no cares could de-stroy: Be there at our wak-ing, and give us, we pray your

2. Lord of all eag-er-ness, Lord of all faith, Whose strong hands were skilled at the plane and the lathe: Be there at our la-bors, and give us, we pray your

3. Lord of all kind-li-ness, Lord of all grace, Your hands swift to wel-come, your arms to em-brace: Be there at our hom-ing, and give us, we pray your

4. Lord of all gen-tle-ness, Lord of all calm, Whose voice is con-tent-ment, whose pres-ence is balm: Be there at our sleep-ing, and give us, we pray your

Jan Struther (1901-53)

SLANE
Irish Folk Melody
Arr. Elise S. Eslinger

bliss   in our   hearts, Lord, at the break of the   day.
strength in our   hearts, Lord, at the noon of the   day.
love   in our   hearts, Lord, at the eve of the   day.
peace in our   hearts, Lord, at the end of the   day.

25 • Jesus in the Morning

1. Je - sus, Je - sus, Je - sus in the morn - ing,
2. Love Him, love Him, love Him in the morn - ing,
3. Serve Him, serve Him, serve Him in the morn - ing,
4. Thank Him, thank Him, thank Him in the morn - ing,
5. Praise Him, praise Him, praise Him in the morn - ing,

Je - sus at the noon - time, Je - sus,
love Him at the noon - time, Love Him,
serve Him at the noon - time, Serve Him,
thank Him at the noon - time, Thank Him,
praise Him at the noon - time, Praise Him,

Je - sus, Je - sus when the sun goes down.
love Him, love Him when the sun goes down.
serve Him, serve Him when the sun goes down.
thank Him, thank Him when the sun goes down.
praise Him, praise Him when the sun goes down.

Traditional

Traditional
Arr. Elise S. Eslinger

26 • Now, on Land and Sea Descending

1. Now, on land and sea des-cend-ing, Brings the night its peace pro-found;
2. Soon as dies the sun-set glo-ry, Stars of heav'n shine out a-bove,
3. Now, our wants and bur-dens leav-ing To God's care who cares for all,
4. As the dark-ness deep-ens o'er us, The e-ter-nal stars a-rise;

Let our ves-per hymn be blend-ing With the ho-ly calm a-round.
Tell-ing still the an-cient sto-ry Their Cre-a-tor's change-less love.
Cease we fear-ing cease we griev-ing: At God's touch our bur-dens fall.
Hope and faith and love rise glo-rious, Shin-ing in the spir-it's skies.

1. Ju-bi-la-te, Ju-bi-la-te, Ju-bi-la-te, A-men!
2. Come re-joice now, raise your voic-es, sing God's prais-es! A-men!
3. Come re-joice now, raise your voic-es, sing God's prais-es! A-men!
4. Ju-bi-la-te, Ju-bi-la-te, Ju-bi-la-te, A-men!

Let our ves-per hymn be blend-ing With the ho-ly calm a-round.
Tell-ing still the an-cient sto-ry Their Cre-a-tor's change-less love.
Cease we fear-ing, cease we griev-ing: At God's touch our bur-dens fall.
Hope and faith and love rise glo-rious, Shin-ing in the spir-it's skies.

Samuel Longfellow, alt.

VESPER HYMN
Attr. Dmitri S. Bortniansky,
Arr. John A. Stevenson

27 • God, Who Made the Earth and Heaven

1. God, who made the earth and heav-en, Dark-ness and light.
2. When the con-stant sun re-turn-ing Un-seals our eyes.

Who the day for toil has giv-en, For rest the night,
May we, born a-new like morn-ing, To la-bor rise;

May Your an-gels guard, de-fend us, Slum-ber sweet Your mer-cy send us.
Fit us for the task that calls us, Let not ease and self en-thrall us.

Ho - ly dreams and hopes at-tend us, All through the night.
Strong through You what-e'er be-fall us, O God most wise!

Reginald Heber, Stanza 1
Frederick L. Hosmer, Stanza 2

AR HYD Y NOS
Traditional Welsh Melody

27A • Day Is Done

Alternate Text

1. Day is done, but Love unfailing Dwells ever here;
   Shadows fall, but hope, prevailing, Calms ev'ry fear.
   Loving Parent, none forsaking, Take our hearts, of Love's own making,
   Watch our sleeping, guard our waking, Be always near!

2. Dark descends, but Light unending Shines through our night;
   You are with us, ever lending New strength to sight;
   One in love, your truth confessing, One in hope of heaven's blessing,
   May we see, in love's possessing, Love's endless light!

3. Eyes will close, but you, unsleeping, Watch by our side;
   Death may come: in Love's safe keeping Still we abide.
   God of love, all evil quelling, Sin forgiving, fear dispelling,
   Stay with us, our hearts indwelling, This eventide!

James Quinn

28 • I Come with Joy

1. I come with joy to meet my Lord, for - giv - en, loved, and free, In awe and won - der to re - call his life laid down for me, his life laid down for me.

2. I come with Chris - tians far and near to find, as all are fed, The new com - mu - ni - ty of love in Christ's com - mu - nion bread, in Christ's com - mu - nion bread.

3. As Christ breaks bread and bids us share each proud di - vi - sion ends. The love that made us makes us one, and stran - gers now are friends, and stran - gers now are friends.

4. And thus with joy we meet our Lord. His pres - ence al - ways near, Is in such friend - ship bet - ter known; we see and praise him here; we see and praise him here.

5. To - geth - er met, to - geth - er bound, we'll go our dif - ferent ways, And as his peo - ple in the world, we'll live and speak his praise, we'll live and speak his praise.

Brian A. Wren

DOVE OF PEACE
Southern Harmony, 1835
Arr. Austin C. Lovelace

29 • Draw Us in the Spirit's Tether

1. Draw us in the Spir-it's te-ther, For when hum-bly
2. As the breth-ren used to gath-er In the Name of
3. All our meals and all our liv-ing Make as sac-ra-

in thy name, Two or three are met to-geth-er, Thou art
Christ to sup, Then with thanks to God the Fa-ther Break the
ments of thee, that by car-ing, help-ing, giv-ing, We may

in the midst of them; Al-le-lu - ia! Al-le-
bread and bless the cup, Al-le-lu - ia! Al-le-
true dis-ci-ples be. Al-le-lu - ia! Al-le-

lu - ia! Touch we now thy gar - ment's hem.
lu - ia! So knit thou our frien - ship up.
lu - ia! We will serve thee faith - ful - ly.

Percy Dearmer (1867-1936)

UNION SEMINARY
Harold Friedell
Adapt. Jet Turner

30 • We Gather at Your Table, Lord

1. We gath - er at your ta - ble, Lord, Be - cause you bid us come.
2. Re - mind us of our sa - cred past, Our roots in Is - rael's soil.
3. We gath - er as your peo - ple, Lord; You call and we must heed.
4. In - to the world a - gain we take Your cov - e - nant of grace.

Our lives, though scat-tered through the week, we now u - nite as one.
Re - fresh us with your pres - ence now As through to - day we toil,
Our pow - er by it - self is weak, It is your strength we need.
Re - freshed by tak - ing time to pause From our own sel - fish pace.

Be - fore us is the bread, the wine, Pre - pare our souls to eat.
And point us toward the fu - ture, Lord, Your King - dom we would know.
Your Spir - it dwell with - in our hearts; Your voice speak loud and clear,
May love be ours and o - ver - flow That all the world may see,

Come join us by your Spir - it, Lord, And make the feast com - plete.
And for our friends a - round us here, Our hearts in love would grow.
And fill us with your power and might As we as - sem - ble here.
That you will be our ho - ly God, And your peo - ple we will be.

William Martin

CLEANSING FOUNTAIN
Early American Tune

31 • Take Our Bread

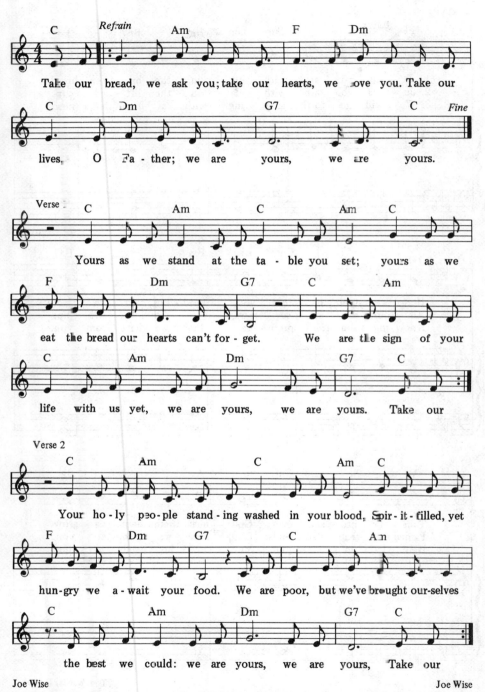

Refrain

Take our bread, we ask you; take our hearts, we love you. Take our lives. O Fa - ther; we are yours, we are yours.

Verse 1

Yours as we stand at the ta - ble you set; yours as we eat the bread our hearts can't for - get. We are the sign of your life with us yet, we are yours, we are yours. Take our

Verse 2

Your ho - ly peo - ple stand - ing washed in your blood, Spir - it - filled, yet hun - gry we a - wait your food. We are poor, but we've brought our-selves the best we could: we are yours, we are yours, Take our

Joe Wise

Joe Wise

32 • Jesus, You Are with Us

1. Je-sus you are with us in the bro-ken bread.
2. Je-sus you are with us in the lift-ed cup.
3. We will go forth sing-ing with a hope that's new.

Here we stand be-fore you, need-ing to be fed.
All our ach-ing sor-rows, to You we lift up.
Know-ing the fresh prom-ise that we have from you.

Take our bro-ken lives, God: heal them, help us grow.
Pained and trou-bled souls, God, here we give to you.
Help us in our jour-ney, lov-ing deeds to do.

Tom Neufer Emswiler

Tom Neufer Emswiler
Arr. Elise S. Eslinger

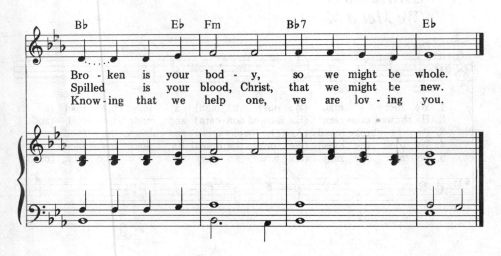

Bro - ken is your bod - y, so we might be whole.
Spilled is your blood, Christ, that we might be new.
Know - ing that we help one, we are lov - ing you.

33 • God Wills a Full Life for Us All

1. God wills a full life for us all, Loves us with ten - der care,
2. The feast is spread for blind and poor; It's spread for you and me,
3. The meal we share binds us to meet Each cap - tive's deep - est need:
4. We leave your ta - ble, now, and seek Christ's spir - it for our days;
5. Thanks be to God for faith re - newed And u - ni - ty re - stored:

Asks us to take the sac - ri - fice Of bro - ken life to share.
God's grace brings light and strength, and sets Life's bro - ken vic - tims free.
For - give us, God, that we have giv'n Love's word but not love's deed.
Help us to live your word of love With deeds that sing your praise.
We go, one world, one fam - i - ly, To live God's lov - ing Word.

Paul R. Gregory

AZMON
Carl G. Glaser
Arr. Lowell Mason

34 • Emmaus
(We Met a Man)

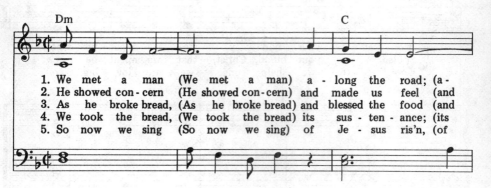

1. We met a man (We met a man) a - long the road; (a -
2. He showed con - cern (He showed con - cern) and made us feel (and
3. As he broke bread, (As he broke bread) and blessed the food (and
4. We took the bread, (We took the bread) its sus - ten - ance; (its
5. So now we sing (So now we sing) of Je - sus ris'n, (of

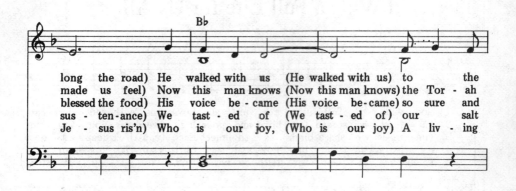

long the road) He walked with us (He walked with us) to the
made us feel) Now this man knows (Now this man knows) the Tor - ah
blessed the food) His voice be - came (His voice be - came) so sure and
sus - ten - ance) We tast - ed of (We tast - ed of) our salt
Je - sus ris'n) Who is our joy, (Who is our joy) A liv - ing

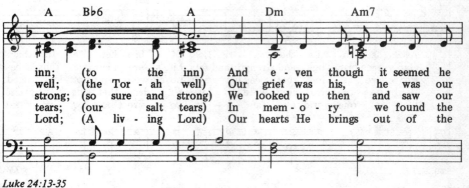

inn; (to the inn) And e - ven though it seemed he
well; (the Tor - ah well) Our grief was his, he was our
strong; (so sure and strong) We looked up then and saw our
tears; (our salt tears) In mem - o - ry we found the
Lord; (A liv - ing Lord) Our hearts He brings out of the

Luke 24:13-35

Judith May Newton

Judith May Newton

did - n't know the trou - ble there had been,
broth - er and there is more that I must tell:
Mas - ter's face, but he did - n't stay there long.
liv - ing fire that con - sumed and pur - i - fied our fears.
pit of death; He has freed us by His Word, *al Coda*

by His Word, by His Word!

35 • Come, My Way, My Truth, My Life

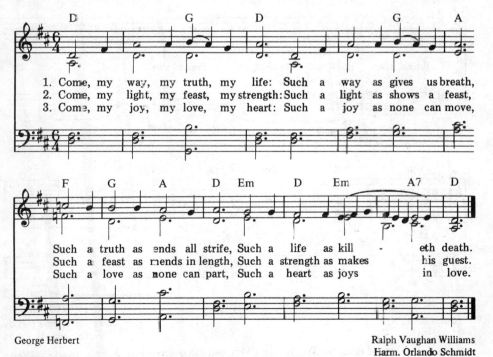

1. Come, my way, my truth, my life: Such a way as gives us breath,
2. Come, my light, my feast, my strength: Such a light as shows a feast,
3. Come, my joy, my love, my heart: Such a joy as none can move,

Such a truth as ends all strife, Such a life as kill - eth death.
Such a feast as mends in length, Such a strength as makes his guest.
Such a love as none can part, Such a heart as joys in love.

George Herbert

Ralph Vaughan Williams
Harm. Orlando Schmidt

Harmony used by permission of Stainer & Bell Ltd, London.

36 • Praise the Lord

Praise the Lord our God, Praise the Lord!

Praise Him from the heights, Praise the Lord!

Praise Him an-gel throngs, Praise the Lord,

Praise God, Praise the Lord!

Richard Bewes

KUM BA YAH
Traditional African melody
Arr. David G. Wilson

36A • In Your Body, Lord

Alternate Text – Communion

1. In your body, Lord, we are one. (3x)
   O Lord, we are one.

2. In this banquet, Lord, we find strength. (3x)
   O Lord, we find strength.

3. Draw us nearer, Lord, each to each. (3x)
   O Lord, each to each.

4. Fill our minds, Lord, with Your peace. (3x)
   O Lord, with Your peace.

5. Undivided, Lord, we shall stand. (3x)
   O Lord, we shall stand.

6. Alleluia, Lord, Allelu. (3x)
   O Lord, Allelu.

Barry Moore

36B • Kum Ba Yah

Alternate Text

1. Kum ba yah, my Lord, Kum ba yah! (3x)
   O Lord, Kum ba yah!

2. Someone's crying, Lord, Kum ba yah! (3x)
   O Lord, Kum ba yah!

3. Someone's singing. . . (3x)
   O Lord, Kum ba yah!

4. Someone's praying. . . (3x)
   O Lord, Kum ba yah!

5. Come by here, my Lord, come by here. (3x)
   O Lord, come by here.

Traditional

37 • Now Let Us from This Table Rise

Alternate text – Communion   (Sing with Tallis' Canon, No. 21.)

1. Now let us from this table rise
   renewed in body, mind, and soul;
   With Christ we die and live again,
   His selfless love has made us whole.

2. With minds alert, upheld by grace,
   to spread the Word in speech and deed,
   We follow in the steps of Christ,
   At one with man *in hope and need.

3. To fill each human house with love,
   it is the sacrament of care;
   The work that Christ began to do
   We humbly pledge ourselves to share.

4. Then grant us courage, Father God,
   To choose again the pilgrim way
   And help us to accept with joy
   The challenge of tomorrow's day.

*May substitute "all."

Fred Kaan

II

SONGS

This section contains a selection of music for which melody lines and guitar chords have been provided. Due to space limitations, no keyboard accompaniments are included, but these certainly may be improvised. The absence of keyboard, however, is sometimes a gift to the worshiping group: the gentle environment evoked by *a capella* singing, or by guitar or Autoharp accompaniment, can be very supportive to participation in prayerful and praise-filled song.

The texts of these songs are primarily responsive in character, yet are full of images and scriptural references. Users of the music may wish to look for ways to add visuals, dance, or simple movement to undergird these images. Utilizing the talents of different persons of varied backgrounds in unique artistic expressions, groups can "match up" a particular musical selection with the talents of the individuals available, always keeping in mind the particular liturgical and community needs of the day.

When the atmosphere is informal, care still should be taken that musical choices are appropriate. Some selections may be used simply for gathering and praise; others may serve as response to the word; and some may actually themselves be sung prayer. Whether the atmosphere is formal or informal, the leader of music seeks to support and guide the group with gentle confidence. Soloists and instrumentalists might best view themselves as servants to the scripture of the day and to the group, seeking always to be "transparent," pointing to God, rather than drawing attention to themselves. Whatever else, the music of the congregation or group is a gift, building the unity and common life in *koinonia* through shared sound, shared focus, shared heartfelt response, shared celebration. Sing with quiet joy!

38 • Glorious in Majesty

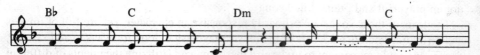

1. Glo - ri - ous in ma - jes - ty, ho - ly in His prais - es,
2. Vic - to - ry he won for us, free - ing us from dark - ness,
3. One in love, as fam - i - ly, liv - ing with each oth - er,

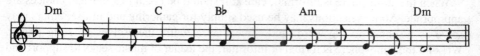

Je - sus, our Sa - vior and our King. Born a man, yet God of old,
dy - ing and ris - ing from the dead. Liv - ing with God now,
glad - ly we share each oth - er's pain. Yet He will not leave us so,

let us all a - dore Him: filled with His Spir - it, let us sing.
yet He is a - mong us: we are the bod - y, He the head.
soon He is re - turn - ing, tak - ing us back with Him to reign.

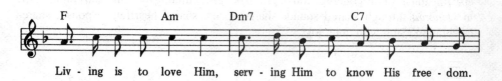

Liv - ing is to love Him, serv - ing Him to know His free - dom.

Come a - long with us to join the praise of Je - sus.

Come to Je - sus now, Go to live His Word re - joic - ing.

*Accompaniment by hand clapping may be effective:

Jeff Cothran

Traditional Jewish melody
Arr. Jeff Cothran

39 • Hosanna

Vigorously

Ho - san - na, Ho - san - na in the high - est.

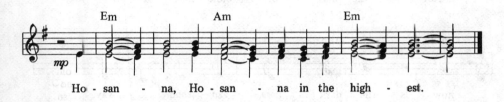

Ho - san - na, Ho - san - na in the high - est.

VERSES

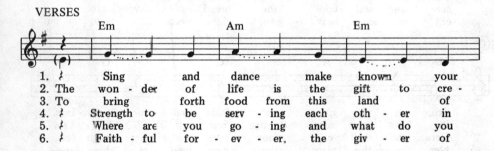

1.	Sing	and	dance	make	known	your
2.	The	won - der	of	life	is	the	gift	to	cre -
3.	To	bring	forth	food	from	this	land	of
4.	Strength to	be	serv - ing	each	oth - er	in
5.	Where are	you	go - ing	and	what	do	you
6.	Faith - ful	for - ev - er,	the	giv - er	of

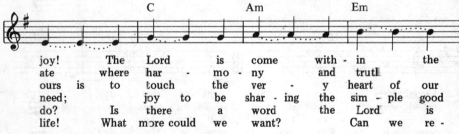

joy!	The	Lord	is	come	with - in	the
ate	where	har - mo - ny	and	truth
ours	is	to	touch	the	ver - y	heart	of	our
need;	joy	to	be	shar - ing	the	sim - ple	good
do?	Is	there	a	word	the	Lord	is
life!	What	more could	we	want?	Can	we	re -

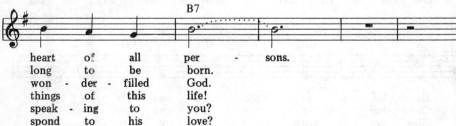

heart	of	all	per - sons.
long	to	be	born.
won - der - filled	God.
things	of	this	life!
speak - ing	to	you?
spond	to	his	love?

Gregory Norbet

Gregory Norbet

From the album *Wherever You Go* © 1972, Gregory Norbet composer, Benedictine Foundation of the State of Vermont, Inc. Used by permission.

40 • Gather Us In
(Here in This Place)

Marty Haugen

Marty Haugen

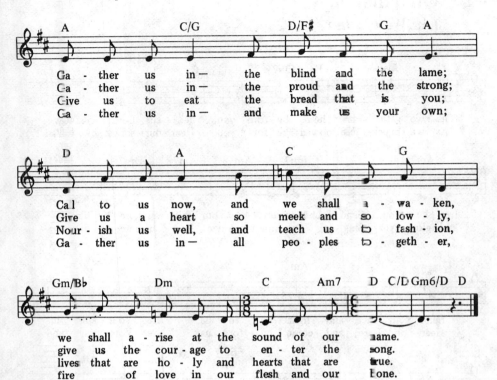

Ga - ther us in — the blind and the lame;
Ca - ther us in — the proud and the strong;
Give us to eat the bread that is you;
Ga - ther us in — and make us your own;

Call to us now, and we shall a - wa - ken,
Give us a heart so meek and so low - ly,
Nour - ish us well, and teach us to fash - ion,
Ga - ther us in — all peo - ples to - geth - er,

we shall a - rise at the sound of our name.
give us the cour - age to en - ter the song.
lives that are ho - ly and hearts that are true.
fire of love in our flesh and our bone.

41 • On This Day
(As We Gather)

VERSES

1. As we gath - er here be - fore you, Je - sus, Lord, we now
2. As we kneel here bowed be - fore you, Hear our songs of praise

im - plore You. Send Your love un - to Your chil-dren here to - day.
and glo - ry— Sing - ing out how much we love You, here to - day.

Send Your grace and light un - to us; Let Your spir - it
Hear, oh Lord, and come be - fore us; Let Your grace and

shine right through us That the world might know Your love in
love re - store us, And have mer - cy on Your chil - dren,

us to - day.
here to - day.

REFRAIN

Come, oh Lord, come now un - to us. Send Your spir - it

to re - new us, And Your love so free - ly giv - en on this day.

William E. Mims

William E. Mims

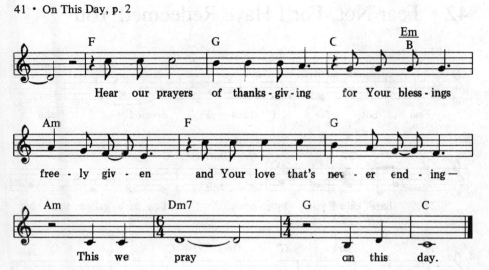

Hear our prayers of thanks-giv-ing for Your bless-ings
free-ly giv-en and Your love that's nev-er end-ing—
This we pray on this day.

42 • Fear Not, For I Have Redeemed You

Isaiah 43, selected verses
Jodi Clark

Jodi Clark
Arr. Patricia Allen

When you walk through the fire you will not be burned;
You whom I called by my Name,
You are my ser-vants for the world to see

I'm mak - ing a way in the wil - der - ness,
To quench their thirst and to strength-en them,

D   D7 |1.-3. G   G7 *D.C.*

The flames shall not con - sume you.
I will gath - er to - geth - er.
I am the Lord, I'm a - mong you.

|4.   *D.C.* |5. G   G7 *D.C.*

And riv - ers to flow in the des - ert.
That they might show forth my praise.

43 • Alleluia
(My Word)

REFRAIN

Al - le - lu - ia, (al - le - lu - ia) al - le - lu - ia, (al - le - lu - ia) al - le-

lu - ia, (al - le - lu - ia) al - le - lu - ia, al - le - lu - ia.

VERSES

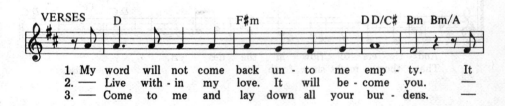

1. My word will not come back un - to me emp - ty. It
2. — Live with - in my love. It will be - come you. —
3. — Come to me and lay down all your bur - dens. —

1. will   be filled   with you. REFRAIN
2. Taste my truth and it will make you free. REFRAIN
3. Rest with me and I will send you on. REFRAIN

Joe Wise   Joe Wise

44 • When You Seek Me

REFRAIN

When you seek Me, you shall find Me; when you seek Me with all your heart. When you seek Me, you shall find Me. I will let you find me.

VERSE 1

1. I know the plans I have in mind for you: plans for peace, not dis-as-ter. I know the plans I have in mind for you: I re-serve a fu-ture full of hope for you. REFRAIN

VERSE 2

2. I have loved you with an ev-er-last-ing love; I am firm and con-stant in My love for you. I will com-fort you as I draw you back to Me. I will turn your sad-ness in-to joy-ful song! REFRAIN

Jeremiah 29:1-14; 31:3, 13
Rev. Carey Landry

Rev. Carey Landry

45 • I Am the Light of the World*

Key: F Capo: 5th Play: C

"I am the light of the world! You peo-ple come and fol-low
me!" If you fol-low and love, You'll learn the mys-ter-y Of
what you were meant to do and be.

1. When the song of the an-gels is stilled,
2. —— To find the lost and lone-ly one,
3. —— To free the pris-'ner from all chains,
4. To bring hope to ev-'ry task you do,

When the star in the sky is gone,
᎐ To heal the bro-ken soul with love,
᎐ To make the pow-er-ful ones care,
᎐ To dance at a ba-by's new birth,

When the kings and the shep-herds Have found their way home,
᎐ To feed the hun-gry chil-dren With warmth and good food,
᎐ To re-build the na-tions With strength of good will,
᎐ To make mu-sic in An old per-son's heart,

The work of Christ-mas is be-gun:
To feel the earth be-low the sky a-bove!
To see God's chil-dren ev-'ry-where!
And sing to the col-ors of the earth!

* In response to a Christmas poem by Howard Thurman

Jim Strathdee   Jim Strathdee

46 • Give Us Your Light

(O Lord, You Are Shining)

Juan Antonio Espinosa
Trans. George F. Lockwood, adapt.

Juan Antonio Espinosa
Arr. Raquel Mora Martinez

47 • Lay Your Hands

REFRAIN

Lay Your hands gent - ly up - on us.

Let their touch ren - der Your peace.

Let them bring Your for - give - ness and heal - ing.

Lay Your hands gent - ly, lay Your hands.

VERSES

1. You were sent to free the bro - ken - heart - ed. You were

sent to give sight to the blind. You de -

sire to heal all our ill - ness - es. Lay Your

hands gent - ly, lay Your hands. REFRAIN

Verse 1: *Isaiah 61:1*
Rev. Carey Landry

Rev. Carey Landry

2. Lord, we come to You through one an-oth-er. Lord, we come to You in our need. Lord, we come to You seek-ing whole-ness. Lay Your hands gent-ly lay Your hands.

LAST REFRAIN

LAST REFRAIN

Lay Your hands gent-ly, up-on us. Let their touch ren-der Your peace. Let them bring Your for-give-ness and heal-ing. Lay Your hands gent-ly, lay Your hands. Lay Your hands gent-ly, lay Your hands.

48 • Weave, Weave

REFRAIN

Weave, weave, weave us to - geth - er. Weave us to - geth - er in

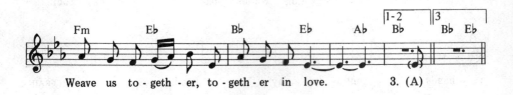

u - ni - ty and love. Weave, weave, weave us to - geth - er,

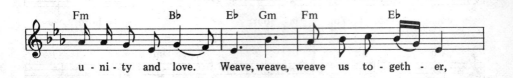

Weave us to - geth - er, to - geth - er in love.　　3. (A)

VERSES

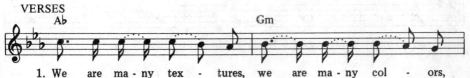

1. We are ma - ny tex - tures, we are ma - ny col - ors,
2. We are dif - f'rent in - stru - ments play - ing our own mel - o - dies
3. Mo - ment a - go we did not know our

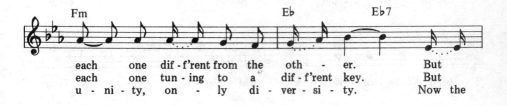

each one dif - f'rent from the oth - er. But
each one tun - ing to a dif - f'rent key. But
u - ni - ty, on - ly di - ver - si - ty. Now the

we are en - twined with one an - oth - er in one great tap - es - try.
we are all play - ing in har - mo - ny in one great sym - pho - ny.
Christ in me greets the Christ in thee in one great fam - i - ly.

Rosemary Crow　　　　　　　　　　　　　　　　　　　　　　Rosemary Crow

49 • Lord, Give Us Your Spirit

REFRAIN

Lord, give us your spir-it, your spir-it that is love.

Lord, fill us with your life, free-ly giv-en for the world.

VERSES

1. Where chil-dren cry let us wipe their tears a-way,
2. Where there is pain let us be your heal-ing hands,
3. Where peo-ple hate let us dwell a-mong them in love,

and where chil-dren fall let us raise them to their feet.
and where there is grief let us com-fort with your love.
and where peo-ple fight let us bind their deep-est wounds.

Sandy Hardyman

Sandy Hardyman

50 • Traveling with God
(One More Step)

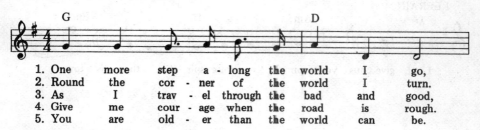

1. One more step a-long the world I go,
2. Round the cor - ner of the world I turn.
3. As I trav - el through the bad and good,
4. Give me cour - age when the road is rough.
5. You are old - er than the world can be.

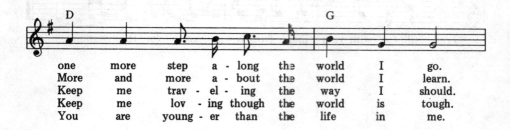

one more step a - long the world I go.
More and more a - bout the world I learn.
Keep me trav - el - ing the way I should.
Keep me lov - ing though the world is tough.
You are young - er than the life in me.

From the old things to the new, Keep me trav - el - ing a-
All the new things that I see You'll be look - ing at a-
Where I see no way to go, you'll be tell - ing me the
Leap and sing in all I do. Keep me trav - el - ing a-
Ev - er old and ev - er new. Keep me trav - el - ing a-

Refrain

long with you. And it's from the old I
long with me.
way, I know.
long with you.
long with you.

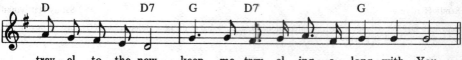

trav - el to the new, keep me trav - el - ing a - long with You.

Sydney Carter   Sydney Carter

DESCANT, VERSE 5 *(vocal or instrumental)*

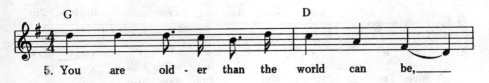

5. You are old-er than the world can be,

You are young-er than the life in me.

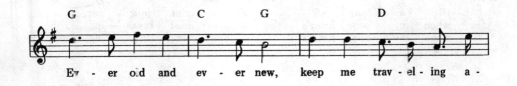

Ev - er old and ev - er new, keep me trav-el-ing a-

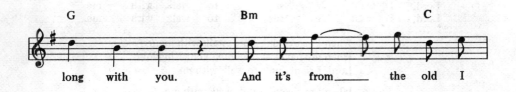

long with you. And it's from the old I

trav-el to the new keep me trav-el-ing a-long with you.

51 • I Want Jesus to Walk with Me

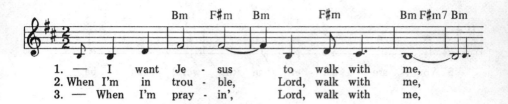

1. — I want Je - sus to walk with me,
2. When I'm in trou - ble, Lord, walk with me,
3. — When I'm pray - in', Lord, walk with me,

— I want Je - sus to walk with me,
when I'm in trou - ble, Lord, walk with me,
— when I'm pray - in', Lord, walk with me,

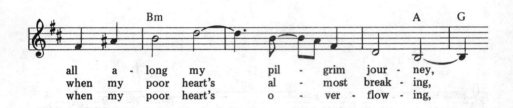

all a - long my pil - grim jour - ney,
when my poor heart's al - most break - ing,
when my poor heart's o - ver - flow - ing,

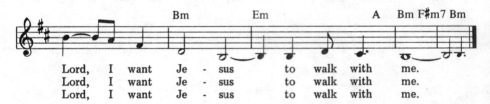

Lord, I want Je - sus to walk with me.
Lord, I want Je - sus to walk with me.
Lord, I want Je - sus to walk with me.

4. When I'm workin', Lord, walk with me, *(repeat)*
   When my hands are building your Kingdom,
   Lord, I want Jesus to walk with me.

5. When I'm singin', Lord, walk with me, *(repeat)*
   When I'm praising all of God's goodness,
   Lord, I want Jesus to walk with me.

6. When I'm lovin', Lord, walk with me, *(repeat)*
   When I'm caring for your children,
   Lord, I want Jesus to walk with me.

7. *Repeat verse 1.*

Traditional

Additional verses, Jim and Jean Strathdee

Traditional Spiritual

Arr. Jim Strathdee

52 • Walk with Me

REFRAIN

Walk with me, I will walk with you. And

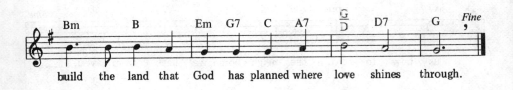

build the land that God has planned where love shines through.

VERSES

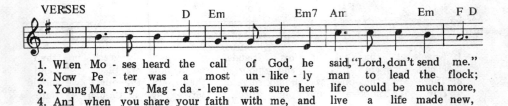

1. When Mo - ses heard the call of God, he said,"Lord, don't send me."
2. Now Pe - ter was a most un - like - ly man to lead the flock;
3. Young Ma - ry Mag - da - lene was sure her life could be much more,
4. And when you share your faith with me, and live a life made new,

But God told Mo - ses,"You're the one to set the peo - ple free."
but Je - sus knew his ho - li - ness and he be - came the rock.
and by her faith she dared to let God's love un - lock the door.
the wit - ness of your faith - ful - ness calls me to walk with you.

*"Barbershop" harmonies are appropriate.
John S. Rice

GLASER
John S. Rice

Written 1981, John S. Rice. Used by permission.

53 • Jesu, Jesu

REFRAIN
Gently

Je - su,   (Je - su)   Je - su,   (Je - su)   fill us with your love, show

us how to serve the neigh - bors we have from you.___

VERSES

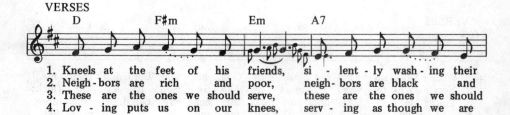

1. Kneels at the feet of his friends, si - lent - ly wash - ing their
2. Neigh - bors are rich and poor, neigh - bors are black and
3. These are the ones we should serve, these are the ones we should
4. Lov - ing puts us on our knees, serv - ing as though we are

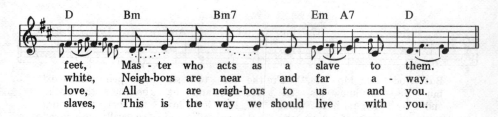

feet,   Mas - ter who acts as a slave to them.
white,   Neigh-bors are near and far a - way.
love,   All are neigh-bors to us and you.
slaves,   This is the way we should live with you.

*Cue-size notes suggest vocal or instrumental improvisation.

John 13:3-5
Ghana text
Trans. Tom Colvin

Ghana Melody
Arr. Elise S. Eslinger

54 • The Servant Song

(Brother,* Let Me Be Your Servant)

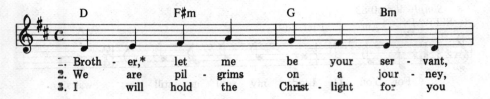

1. Broth - er,* let me be your ser - vant,
2. We are pil - grims on a jour - ney,
3. I will hold the Christ - light for you

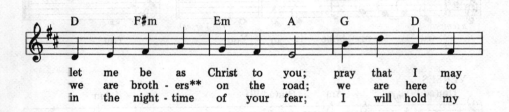

let me be as Christ to you; pray that I may
we are broth - ers** on the road; we are here to
in the night - time of your fear; I will hold my

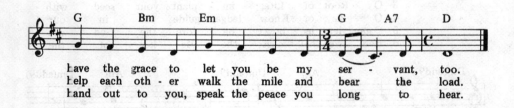

have the grace to let you be my ser - vant, too.
help each oth - er walk the mile and bear the load.
hand out to you, speak the peace you long to hear.

4. I will weep when you are weeping;
When you laugh I'll laugh with you.
I will share your joy and sorrow
'Til we've seen this journey through.

5. When we sing to God in heaven
We shall find such harmony,
Born of all we've known together
Of Christ's love and agony.

* or Pilgrim
** or trav'lers

Richard Gillard

Richard Gillard
Arr. Betty Pulkingham

55 • My Soul in Stillness Waits
(For You, O Lord)

Simply ♩ = 60-63

REFRAIN *mp*

For You, O Lord, my soul in still - ness waits,

Last time to Coda ⊕ — ⊕ CODA — *a tempo* — *Fine*

tru - ly my hope is in You. *(to Verses)* You.

VERSES

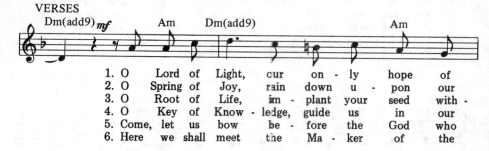

1. O Lord of Light, our on - ly hope of
2. O Spring of Joy, rain down u - pon our
3. O Root of Life, im - plant your seed with -
4. O Key of Know - ledge, guide us in our
5. Come, let us bow be - fore the God who
6. Here we shall meet the Ma - ker of the

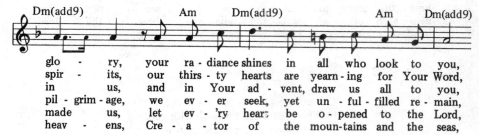

glo - ry, your ra - diance shines in all who look to you,
spir - its, our thirs - ty hearts are yearn - ing for Your Word,
in us, and in Your ad - vent, draw us all to you,
pil - grim - age, we ev - er seek, yet un - ful - filled re - main,
made us, let ev - 'ry heart be o - pened to the Lord,
heav - ens, Cre - a - tor of the moun - tains and the seas,

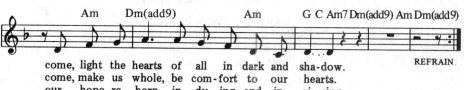

come, light the hearts of all in dark and sha - dow.
come, make us whole, be com - fort to our hearts.
our hope re - born in dy - ing and in ri - sing.
o - pen to us the path - way of Your peace.
for we are all the peo - ple of His hand.
Lord of the stars, and pres - ent to us now.

REFRAIN

Marty Haugen

Marty Haugen

56 • The Gift of Love
(Though I May Speak)

1. Though I may speak with brav - est fire,
2. Though I may give all I pos - sess,
3. Come, Spir - it, come our hearts con - trol,

and have the gift to all in - spire,
and striv - ing so my love pro - fess,
our spir - its long to be made whole.

And have not love; my words are vain;
But not be giv'n — by love with - in,
Let in - ward love — guide ev - ery deed;

as sound - ing brass, and hope - less gain.
the prof - it soon turns strange - ly thin.
by this we wor - ship, and are freed.

1 Corinthians 13
Hal H. Hopson

American Folk Tune
Adapt. Hal H. Hopson

57 • Song of Shalom
(When We Are Living)

Not too fast

1. When we are liv - ing, it is in Christ Je - sus,
2. God sent Christ Je - sus to be our Sha - lom.
3. To pain and sor - row Christ brings Sha - lom.
4. Sha - lom to you, now, Sha - lom, my friends.

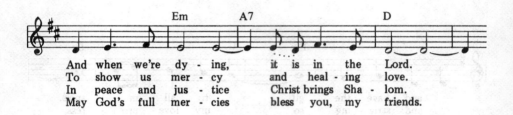

And when we're dy - ing, it is in the Lord.
To show us mer - cy and heal - ing love.
In peace and jus - tice Christ brings Sha - lom.
May God's full mer - cies bless you, my friends.

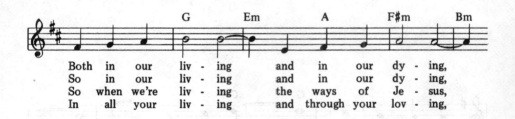

Both in our liv - ing and in our dy - ing,
So in our liv - ing and in our dy - ing,
So when we're liv - ing the ways of Je - sus,
In all your liv - ing and through your lov - ing,

We be - long to God, We be - long to God.
Christ is our Sha - lom, Christ is our Sha - lom.
We are God's Sha - lom, We are God's Sha - lom.
Christ be your Sha - lom, Christ be your Sha - lom.

CODA *Last time only*

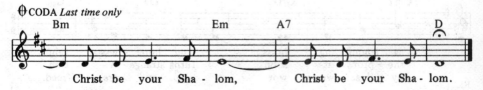

Christ be your Sha - lom, Christ be your Sha - lom.

v. 1, Anonymous Mexican source based on *Romans 14:8-9*   Mexican Melody
v. 2-4, Elise S. Eslinger

58 • We Are the Church
(I Am the Church)

REFRAIN

I am the church, you are the church! We are the church to-geth-er!

All who fol-low Je-sus, All a-round the world! Yes, we're the church to-geth-er.

VERSES

Freely

1. The church is not a build-ing, The church is not a stee-ple,
2. We're man-y kinds of peo-ple With man-y kinds of fac-es,
3. Some-times the church is march-ing, Some-times it's brave-ly burn-ing,
4. And when the peo-ple gath-er There's sing-ing and there's pray-ing,
5. At Pen-te-cost some peo-ple Re-ceived the Ho-ly Spir-it
6. I count if I am nine-ty, Or nine, or just a ba-by;

The church is not a rest-ing place, the church is a peo-ple!
All col-ors and all ag-es, too, from All times and plac-es.
Some-times it's rid-ing, some-times hid-ing, Al-ways it's learn-ing,
There's laugh-ing and there's cry-ing some-times, All of it say-ing:
And told the Good News through the world to All who would hear it.
There's one thing I am sure a-bout and I don't mean may-be:

Richard Avery
and Donald Marsh

Richard Avery
and Donald Marsh

59 • Is There Anybody Here?

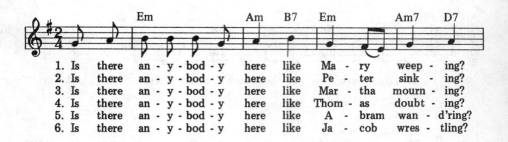

1. Is there an-y-bod-y here like Ma-ry weep-ing?
2. Is there an-y-bod-y here like Pe-ter sink-ing?
3. Is there an-y-bod-y here like Mar-tha mourn-ing?
4. Is there an-y-bod-y here like Thom-as doubt-ing?
5. Is there an-y-bod-y here like A-bram wan-d'ring?
6. Is there an-y-bod-y here like Ja-cob wres-tling?

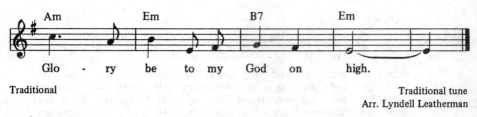

Call on my Je-sus and He'll draw nigh. He'll draw nigh.

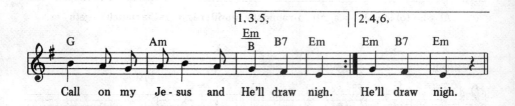

Glo - ry, glo - ry, glo - ry, glo - ry,

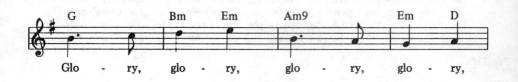

Glo - ry be to my God on high.

Traditional

Traditional tune
Arr. Lyndell Leatherman

60 • Give Me Joy in My Heart

Traditional

Traditional

61 • Livin' in Love
(Once I Walked in Darkness)

VERSES

1. Once I walked in dark-ness, a-fraid to count the cost,
2. God, who made the earth and the heav-ens up a-bove,
3. When I think of all of the won-ders of God's grace,

hop - ing some - thing bet - ter could be found.
Lord, who made the sky and the sea,
When I think of all that Christ gave,

Then I met the Lord of life, and I knew that I was lost;
You're the one who said, "Put your life in - to my hands,
Then I know that we will see the glo - ry in His face.

he set my sights on heav - en and my feet on high - er ground.
and I will give new life and you will live a - bun-dant-ly."
He gave His life up - on the cross, each wan-d'ring child to save.

REFRAIN

And now we're liv - in' in love that sets us free, we're

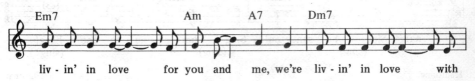

liv - in' in love for you and me, we're liv - in' in love with

Ruth Ann Parish   Ruth Ann Parish

Christ e - ter - nal - ly. And now we're

liv - in' in love that sets us free we're liv - in in love for

you and me, we're liv - in' in love, with Him e - ter - nal - ly.

*At end: Amaj7.

62 • Gifts of Love
(Gifts of Healing)

REFRAIN:

Gifts of heal - ing, gifts of kind - ness,

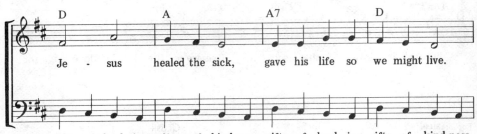

Je - sus healed the sick, gave his life so we might live.

gifts of heal - ing, gifts of kind-ness, gifts of heal - ing, gifts of kind-ness,

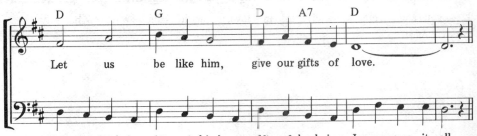

Let us be like him, give our gifts of love.

gifts of heal - ing, gifts of kind-ness, gifts of heal - ing, Je - sus gave it all.

VERSES:

1. Je - sus healed the sick, the lame; crip - pled ones did walk a - gain.
2. Je - sus died up - on the cross; man - y thought it was a loss.
3. Let us fol - low Je - sus' way: giv - ing gifts of love each day.

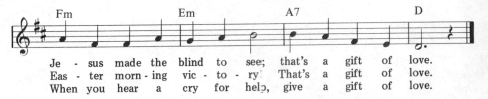

Je - sus made the blind to see; that's a gift of love.
Eas - ter morn - ing vic - to - ry. That's a gift of love.
When you hear a cry for help, give a gift of love.

Art Allen

Art Allen

63 • My Name
(Love Is My Name)

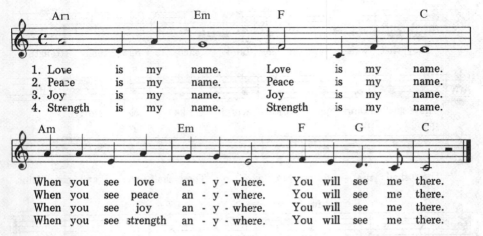

An	Em	F	C

1. Love is my name. Love is my name.
2. Peace is my name. Peace is my name.
3. Joy is my name. Joy is my name.
4. Strength is my name. Strength is my name.

Am	Em	F G	C

When you see love an - y - where. You will see me there.
When you see peace an - y - where. You will see me there.
When you see joy an - y - where. You will see me there.
When you see strength an - y - where. You will see me there.

Barbara Neighbors   Barbara Neighbors

64 • Come to Me

ANTIPHON
(♩.=40)

Come to me, all you who thirst: Come, and life shall be yours.

Seek and you will find, knock and the door shall be o - pened.

VERSES: (for equal voices)   (to ANT.)

1. Take my yoke up - on you and you will find rest for your souls.
2. Seek in faith the King-dom, and all will be giv - en to you.
3. Trust in me and fear not: come, drink from the foun-tain of life.

Matthew 6:33; 7:7; 11:29
John 4:14; 7:37-38
Becket Senchur

Becket Senchur

65 • They That Wait upon the Lord

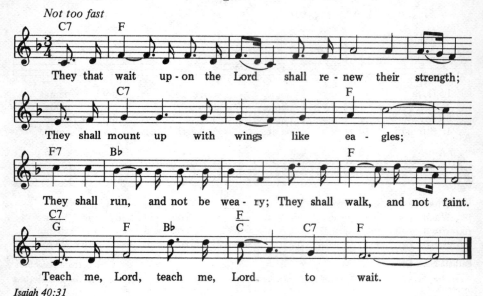

Not too fast

They that wait up-on the Lord shall re-new their strength;

They shall mount up with wings like ea - gles;

They shall run, and not be wea - ry; They shall walk, and not faint.

Teach me, Lord, teach me, Lord to wait.

Isaiah 40:31
Stuart Hamblen

Stuart Hamblen

66 • Seek Ye First

*☐1 Rich and broad

1. Seek ye first the king - dom of God and its right-eous - ness,
2. Ask, and it shall be giv-en un - to you, Seek, and ye shall find.

and all these things shall be add -ed un - to you;
Knock, and the door shall be o-pened un - to you; Al - le - lu, al - le - lu - ia.

☐2 REFRAIN *(Descant):*

Al - le - lu - ia, al - le - lu - ia, al - le - lu - ia, al - le - lu, al - le - lu - ia.

* ☐1 and ☐2 may be sung simultaneously.

v. 1, *Matthew 6:33* (King James Version)
Karen Lafferty
v. 2, *Matthew 7:7* (King James Version)
(Anonymous, not part of original)

Karen Lafferty

III

RESPONSES AND ROUNDS

Recent renewal of worship has affirmed repeatedly the role of the congregation in the action of the liturgy. This section particularly highlights the congregation's musical role in worship, providing varied and accessible alternatives for those places of response and acclamation: greeting, blessing, benediction, praise, petition, doxology, Amen, Alleluia!

The use of rounds is especially helpful in building an environment of sound (full and beautiful!) with no accompaniment necessary. Rounds in this section indicate by number the entry of voices. These rounds and the responses are easily taught by rote, and with repeated use will become "at home" in the repertoire of the congregation or group. Many persons sing more freely when reading words or music isn't necessary; thus, broader participation by all ages is possible. Music is captured only partially by notations on paper, just as scripture is more than words. Let the Spirit move to evoke spontaneous bursts of sound out of a gradually growing repertoire of short and simple songs.

Enjoy the fellowship-building, unity-enhancing, joy-filled responses in this section.

67 • Jubilate Deo

Voices:

*Ju - bi - la - te De - o, Ju - bi - la - te De - o, A - le - lu - ia.

*Accompaniment *(optional):*

(Fine)

*If accompaniment is used, repeat vocal part four times.

Traditional

Taizé Community
Arr. Jacques Berthier

68 • Gloria in Excelsis

Glo - ri - a, glo - ri - a, in ex - cel - sis De - o!

Glo - ri - a, glo - ri - a, al - le - lu - ia, al - le - lu - ia!

Traditional

Taizé Community
Arr. Jacques Berthier

69 • Gloria Patri
(Glory Be to the Father)

Glo-ry be to the Fa-ther and to the Son, and to the Spir-it, three in One. As it was in the be-gin-ning and shall for-ev-er be, our world with-out end. A-men.

Traditional Liturgical Text
Adapt. Judy Loehr

BLACKSTONE
Judy Loehr

70 • Agnus Dei
(Jesus, Lamb of God)

Je - sus, Lamb of God: have mer - cy on us.

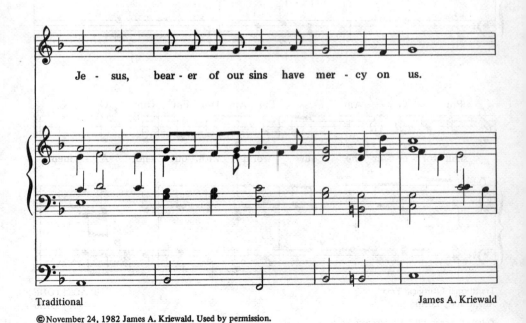

Je - sus, bear - er of our sins have mer - cy on us.

Traditional

James A. Kriewald

Je - sus, Re - deem - er of the world: Give us your Peace.

71 • Alleluia *(Eight-fold)*

Sung in quiet adoration

1. Al - le - lu - ia, Al - le - lu - ia,
(Alto) Al - le - lu - ia, Al - le - lu - ia,

Al - le - lu - ia, Al - le - lu - ia, Al - le - lu - ia,
(Alto) Al - le - lu - ia,

Al - le - lu - ia, Al - le - lu - ia. lu - ia.

Additional Verses

2. Blessed Jesus. . .
3. Precious Savior. . .
4. My redeemer, . . .
5. Jesus Christ is Lord. . .
6. Al - le - lu - ia,

Also, verses may be improvised:

God is with us; (Christmas)
Lord, we love you; (Lent)
He is risen; (Easter)

Anonymous

Anonymous
Arr. Betty Pulkingham

DESCANTS

2. Bless - ed Je - sus, Bless - ed Je - sus, Bless - ed

Je - sus, Bless - ed Je - sus, Bless - ed Je - sus,

Bless - ed, Bless - ed, Bless - ed, Bless - ed Je - sus.

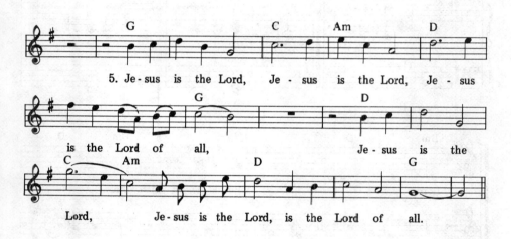

5. Je - sus is the Lord, Je - sus is the Lord, Je - sus

is the Lord of all, Je - sus is the

Lord, Je - sus is the Lord, is the Lord of all.

6. Al - le - lu - ia, Al - le - lu - ia, Al - le -

lu - ia, Al - le - lu - ia, Al - le - lu,

Al - le - lu - ia, Al - le - lu - ia.

72 • Sing Hallelujah to the Lord

Linda Stassen   Linda Stassen

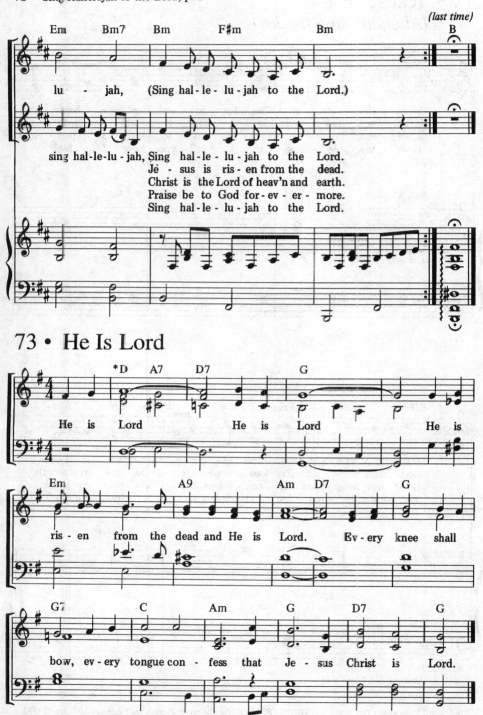

(last time)

lu - jah, (Sing hal-le-lu-jah to the Lord.)

sing hal-le-lu - jah, Sing hal - le - lu-jah to the Lord.
Je - sus is ris - en from the dead.
Christ is the Lord of heav'n and earth.
Praise be to God for - ev - er - more.
Sing hal - le - lu - jah to the Lord.

73 • He Is Lord

He is Lord He is Lord He is

ris - en from the dead and He is Lord. Ev-ery knee shall

bow, ev - ery tongue con - fess that Je - sus Christ is Lord.

*Guitar chords not for use with keyboard accompaniment.
Anonymous, based on *Philippians 2:10-11*

Anonymous

74 • Jesus, Jesus

(Alleluia! Sing for Joy)

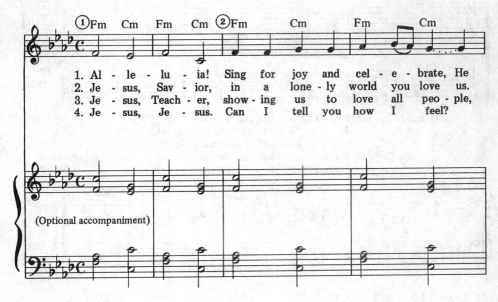

1. Al - le - lu - ia! Sing for joy and cel - e - brate, He
2. Je - sus, Sav - ior, in a lone - ly world you love us.
3. Je - sus, Teach - er, show - ing us to love all peo - ple,
4. Je - sus, Je - sus. Can I tell you how I feel?

(Optional accompaniment)

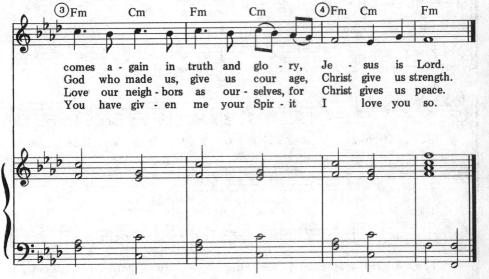

comes a - gain in truth and glo - ry, Je - sus is Lord.
God who made us, give us cour - age, Christ give us strength.
Love our neigh - bors as our - selves, for Christ gives us peace.
You have giv - en me your Spir - it I love you so.

V. 1-3, Alf Siemens and Tom Graff   T. Ravenscroft
V. 4, Anonymous   Arr. Elise S. Eslinger

75 • Thank You, Lord

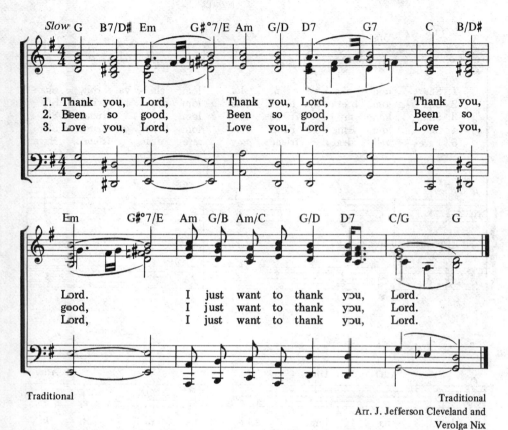

1. Thank you, Lord, Thank you, Lord, Thank you,
2. Been so good, Been so good, Been so
3. Love you, Lord, Love you, Lord, Love you,

Lord.   I just want to thank you, Lord.
good,   I just want to thank you, Lord.
Lord,   I just want to thank you, Lord.

Traditional

Traditional
Arr. J. Jefferson Cleveland and
Verolga Nix

76 • Praise for Bread
(Morning Has Come)

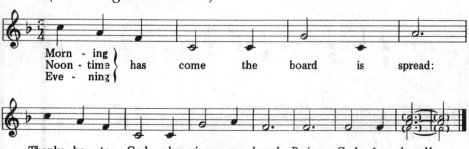

Morn - ing }
Noon - time } has come the board is spread:
Eve - ning }

Thanks be to God, who gives us bread. Praise God for bread!

Albert R. Ledoux, alt.

From NORFOLK CHIMES
Arr. Clarence Dickinson

77 • Shalom Chaverim

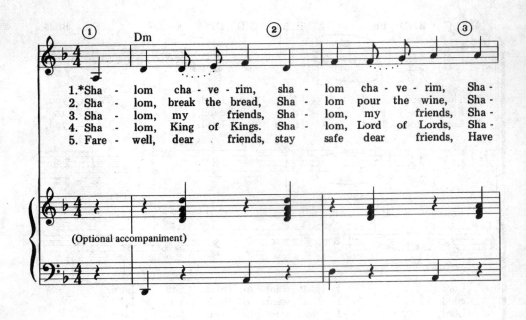

1.*Sha - lom cha - ve - rim, sha - lom cha - ve - rim, Sha-
2. Sha - lom, break the bread, Sha - lom pour the wine, Sha-
3. Sha - lom, my friends, Sha - lom, my friends, Sha-
4. Sha - lom, King of Kings. Sha - lom, Lord of Lords, Sha-
5. Fare - well, dear friends, stay safe dear friends, Have

(Optional accompaniment)

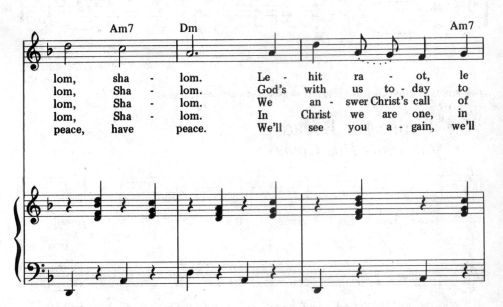

lom, sha - lom. Le - hit ra - ot, le
lom, Sha - lom. God's with us to - day to
lom, Sha - lom. We an - swer Christ's call of
lom, Sha - lom. In Christ we are one, in
peace, have peace. We'll see you a - gain, we'll

*Choose verses appropriate to occasion.
Various sources
Verse 5, trans. Roger Deschner

Traditional Hebrew Melody
Arr. Elise S. Eslinger

hit - ra - ot, Sha - lom, Sha - lom.
show us the way, Sha - lom, Sha - lom.
ser - vice to all, Sha - lom, Sha - lom.
Him we are whole, Sha - lom, Sha - lom.
see you a - gain. Have peace, have peace.

78 • The Spirit in Me

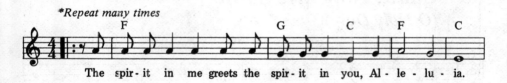

*Repeat many times

The spir-it in me greets the spir-it in you, Al - le - lu - ia.

God's in us and we're in God, Al - le - lu - ia. ia.

* Chant these words as a greeting to each other, during communion, or at the close of the service. Let the volume rise and fall as it will, that the chant sings you rather than you sing the chant. Note: The East Indians greet each other by raising both hands in a gesture of respect. Implicit in the gesture is the idea that "the spirit in me greets the spirit in you."

Jim Strathdee   Jim Strathdee

79 • Spirit of the Living God

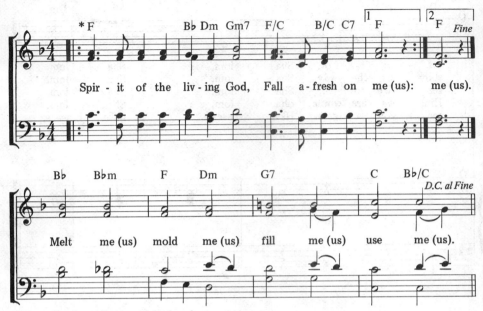

Spir - it of the liv - ing God, Fall a - fresh on me (us): me (us).

Melt me (us) mold me (us) fill me (us) use me (us).

*Guitar chords not for use with keyboard accompaniment.

Daniel Iverson

Daniel Iverson
Arr. Philip S. O'Dell

80 • Spirit, Now Live in Me
(O Holy Dove)

1. O ho - ly Dove of God de - scend - ing, You are the love that knows no end - ing,
2. O ho - ly Wind of God now blow - ing, You are the seed that God is sow - ing,
3. O ho - ly Rain of God now fall - ing, You make the Word of God en - thral - ling,
4. O ho - ly Flame of God now burn - ing, You are the pow'r of Christ re - turn - ing,

all of our shat - tered dreams you're mend - ing: Spir - it, now live in me.
you are the life that starts us grow - ing: Spir - it, now live in me.
you are the in - ner voice now call - ing: Spir - it, now live in me.
you are the an - swer to our yearn - ing: Spir - it, now live in me.

Brian Jeffery Leech

Brian Jeffery Leech

81 • Create Us New
(We Lift Our Hearts)

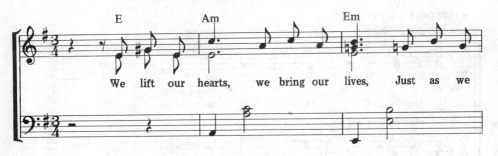

We lift our hearts, we bring our lives, Just as we

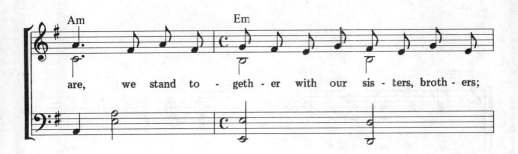

are, we stand to - geth - er with our sis - ters, broth - ers;

Lord, cre - ate us new in your Spir - it.

Judith May Newton

Judith May Newton

82 • Ubi Caritas

Where charity and love are found, God is there.

Two Parts

Third Part (Instrumental or Vocal) *ad lib.*

U - bi ca - ri - tas et a - mor,

U - bi ca - ri - tas De - us i - bi est.

*Sung continuously by the community before, during and after the verses.

ACCOMPANIMENT
Keyboard or Instruments

Traditional Text

Taizé Community
arr. Jacques Berthier

** VERSES for soloists or small mixed choir.

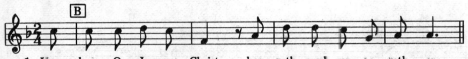

1. Your love, O Je - sus Christ, has gath - ered us to - geth - er.

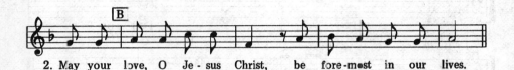

2. May your love, O Je - sus Christ, be fore - most in our lives.

3. Let us love one an - oth - er as God has loved us.

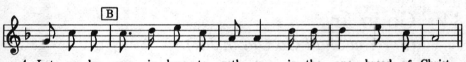

4. Let us be one in love to - geth - er in the one bread of Christ.

5. The love of God in Je - sus Christ bears e - ter - nal joy.

6. The love of God in Je - sus Christ will nev - er have an end.

**Soloists enter at B in the ostinato response.

83 • Doxology and Amen
(Amen, Praise the Father)

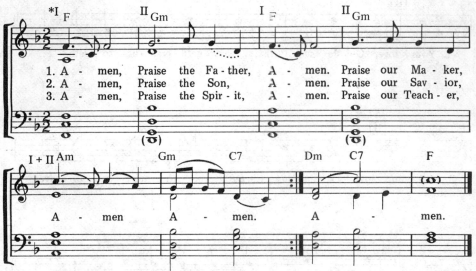

1. A - men, Praise the Fa - ther, A - men. Praise our Ma - ker,
2. A - men, Praise the Son, A - men. Praise our Sav - ior,
3. A - men, Praise the Spir - it, A - men. Praise our Teach - er,

A - men A - men. A - men.

*May be sung by two groups, or leader and congregation.

Leng Loh

Leng Loh
Arr. Elise S. Eslinger

Music and words © 1983 by Leng Loh. Used by permission. Arrangement © 1985 by The Upper Room.

84 • Go in Joy
(For You Shall Go Out in Joy)

Gently, with freedom

For you shall go out in joy and be led forth in peace:

The moun - tains and the hills shall break forth in - to sing - ing.

An ending song for singers, dancers, and optional rhythm instruments. Each section may be added at two or three phrase intervals. Depending upon the number of people and the length of song desired, the sequence may build up to I, II, III, IV and then reduce back to I alone. Section IV is spoken, with two hand claps, and may be omitted by the congregation and done by the choir or dancers.

Isaiah 55:12
Don E. Saliers

Don E. Saliers

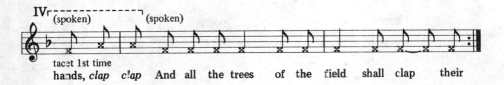

IV (spoken) (spoken)

tacet 1st time
hands, *clap clap* And all the trees of the field shall clap their

85 • Peace I Leave You

Peace I leave you, peace I leave you, go now and spread the word,

Tell the good news you've heard: God lives in love.

Traditional, based on *John 14:27*   Israeli Melody

Copyright © Choristers Guild, reprinted by permission.

86 • Go Now in Peace

Go now in peace. Go now in peace, May the love of

God sur - round you ev - 'ry - where, ev - 'ry - where you may go.

Natalie Sleeth   Natalie Sleeth

From SUNDAY SONGBOOK, by Natalie Sleeth, copyright © 1976 by Hinshaw Music, Inc., Chapel Hill, NC 27514. Used by permission.

85. Place I leave You

86. Go Now in Peace

IV

PSALMS, A SELECTION

The Psalms—truly the heart of the Christian's daily prayer—are represented in this section by a number of original as well as previously published settings of varied types and musical styles. The decision to include a variety of approaches rather than a single musical style was made in order to introduce multiple possibilities to persons not used to singing Psalms at all. Once a community is comfortable with forms of sung prayers, leaders will want to explore further possibilities and resources.

The overall approach to the Psalms is, of course, that they are meant to be sung! Included are a few metrical and through-composed settings. but most examples are responscrial in character (leader/cantor and congregation). Reading is sometimes interspersed with singing in order to encourage participation and to offer variety. In the daily liturgies. Psalms certainly may be chosen for reading without music when desired. Creativity is encouraged, but musical settings and styles of singing are best when faithfully serving the texts of the Psalms and the environment of prayer.

The leader or cantor has a special role. The singing of the Psalm text is not primarily a vocal performance but more a musical offering of the text on behalf of the whole congregation. It is not necessary to be a polished soloist in order to pray the Psalms as an effective cantor. Take time to let the rhythm, poetry, and emotion of the text provide guidance and inspiration.

We are indebted to the excellent new translation of the Psalter by Dr. Gary Chamberlain, whose work provided texts for many of the Psalms in this section. In the daily liturgies. other translations may be chosen, of course. Silence is desirable after a Psalm is prayed in the daily liturgies; this may be followed by a Psalm prayer which gathers images from the Psalm, applying it to the life of the gathered people. Several Psalm prayers are included as examples in this section.

The "why" of the Psalter in Christian prayer today is affirmed. celebrated, and explored in resources listed below. That "why" is an important matter indeed: the images and emotions of the Psalter summarize scripture, lead us deeply into the salvation experience of God's people in history, and offer us the unique opportunity to "enter" the mind of Christ who prayed Psalms in all parts of his life and ministry. The God who wills *shalom* for all creation hears in our community prayer the human attitudes of praise, trust, petition, honest anger and pain, true lament, thanksgiving, and rejoicing. The Psalms are formative to our vocabulary, our grammar of praise and prayer, as we offer ourselves wholly to the Holy One.

Additional Resources:

Chamberlain, Gary, trans. *The Psalms: A New Translation for Prayer and Worship.* Nashville: The Upper Room. 1984.

————. *Psalms for Singing.* Nashville: The Upper Room, 1984.

Hawkins, Thomas R. *The Unsuspected Power of the Psalms.* Nashville: The Upper Room, 1984.

87 • Psalm 1
(Happy Are They)

ANTIPHON
Congregation:

Hap-py are they who de-light, who de-light in the Word of God.

VERSES 1-5
Leader:

1. Hap - py in-deed are they who re - fuse the way of the
2. Joy shall be in the hearts of those who de-light in the
3. They are like green trees that grow by clear flow-ing
4. Thus it is not so, not so with ev - il
5. God up - holds the just, God knows the way of the

ev - il; Nor walk the road of the
word of God; For they con - sume that
wa - ters, They bear their fruit in due
do - ers, They blow like chaff in the
righ - teous, but the ev - il ones shall

Trans. Hal H. Hopson

Hal H. Hopson

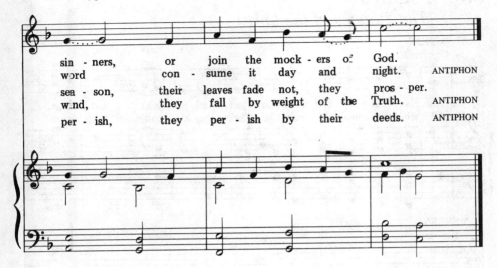

sin - ners,   or   join   the   mock - ers of   God.
word   con - sume it   day   and   night.   ANTIPHON

sea - son,   their leaves fade not,   they   pros - per.   ANTIPHON
wind,   they   fall   by weight of the Truth.   ANTIPHON

per - ish,   they   per - ish by   their   deeds.   ANTIPHON

87A • Psalm Prayer

Teach us your ways, God of Wisdom,
   for you are righteous and just.
Plant your Word in our hearts, watering it
   from the streams of your everflowing mercy,
   that it may blossom and produce in us
   the fruit which is a blessing to you
   and pleasing in your sight. *Amen.*

                    Douglas Mills

88 • Psalm 19
(The Statutes of the Lord)

ANTIPHON
Congregation:

I. The stat - utes of the Lord are just, and re - joice the heart.
II. All wis - dom shall be ours in Christ, sing his truth with joy.

VERSES
Leader:

1. The law of the Lord is perfect, it re -
   The statutes of the Lord are just, and re -

2. The fear of the Lord is holy, en -
   They are more precious than gold, more than a -

3. By them your servant is guided, in keeping them there is
   Above all, keep your servant from foolish pride, let it not

4. Let the words of my mouth, the

news the soul; The rule of the Lord is
joice the heart; The command of the Lord shines

dur - ing for - ever; The decrees of the Lord are
bun - dant, pure gold. The word of the Lord is sweeter than

great re - ward. Who can know all the offences?
rule o - ver me; Then shall I be whole, and

thoughts of my heart, find favor before you, O

Antiphon I: Psalm 19:8a
Antiphon II: Colossians 3:16
Hal H. Hopson

Hal H. Hopson

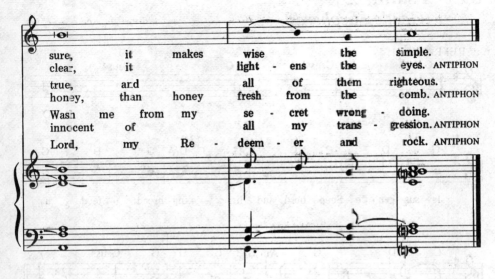

sure,   it   makes   wise   the   simple.
clear,   it   light - ens   the   eyes. ANTIPHON

true,   and   all   of   them   righteous.
honey,   than   honey   fresh   from   the   comb. ANTIPHON

Wash   me   from   my   se - cret   wrong - doing.
innocent   of   all   my   trans - gression. ANTIPHON

Lord,   my   Re - deem - er   and   rock. ANTIPHON

88A • Psalm Prayer

Night and day, all creation declares your glory,
    holy God.
Yet you call us into covenant
    and reveal your will for our lives.
Your perfect instruction renews life;
    your commands can be trusted.
In humility may we serve you, O Lord,
    our rock and our redeemer. *Amen.*

Richard Eslinger

89 • Psalm 23
(Gentle Shepherd)

VERSE 2:

You have pre-pared me a ban-quet   in the sight of my foes.

My   head   you have a-noint-ed with pre - cious   oil,

and my   cup   is o - ver - flow - ing.   O

VERSE 3:

Sure-ly good-ness and kind-ness   shall fol-low me all my days.

In   the Lord's   own   house shall   I   dwell

for - ev - er and ev - er.   O

89A • Psalm Prayer

Blessed are you, Lord Jesus Christ,
Good Shepherd of your Church!
In our baptism you anointed us
with the oil of salvation,
and in the eucharist you spread before us
the table of your heavenly bread.
Lead us by your goodness and kindness
through the dark valley of death
to the day when we will dwell forever
in the house of your Father. *Amen*

Lucien Deiss

90 • Psalm 23
(My Shepherd, You Supply My Need)

1. My shep-herd, you sup-ply my need; and
Yah-weh is your name. In pas-tures fresh you
make me feed, be-side the liv-ing stream. You

2. When I walk through the shades of death, your
pres-ence is my stay; One word of your sup-
port-ing breath drives all my fears a-way. Your

3. The sure pro-vis-ions of my God at-
tend me all my days; O may your house be
my a-bode, and all my work be praise! There

Isaac Watts
Adapt. Mary Ruth Coffman

RESIGNATION
William Walker's *Southern Harmony*
Arr. Sister Theophane Hytrek

bring my wan - d'ring spir - it back when I for
hard, in sight of all my foes, does still my
would I find a set - tled rest [while oth - ers

sake your ways, And lead me for your
ta - ble spread; My cup with bless - ings
go and come), No more a stran - ger,

mer - cy's sake in paths of truth and grace.
o - ver - flows, your oil a - noints my head.
nor a guest; but like a child at home.

91 • Psalm 23
(Your Goodness and Love)

ANTIPHON

Your good-ness and love pur-sue me, my shep-herd, my Lord.

VERSES

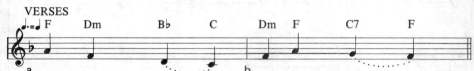

Lord, my shepherd, there's nothing I lack. In fresh pastures you let me lie down... (etc.)

Trans. Gary Chamberlain   Jane Marshall

a Lord, my shepherd, there's nothing I lack.

 b In fresh pastures you let me lie down;

a You lead me beside quiet waters;

 b You restore me to life.   ANTIPHON

a In order to show who you are,

 b You guide me in paths that are right,

a Even walking through dark valleys,

 b I have no fear of harm.

a For you yourself are with me;

 b Your rod and staff reassure me.   ANTIPHON

a Right in front of my foes,

 b You lay out a feast for me.

a You anoint my head with oil,

 b My cup is overflowing.   ANTIPHON

a Goodness and love pursue me

 b Every day of my life;

a God's house will be my home

 b As long as I may live.   ANTIPHON

Trans. Gary Chamberlain

92 • Psalm 30
(You Have Turned Our Sadness)

ANTIPHON

Congregation

(voices) You have turned our sad - ness in -
(my)

Introduction

to a joy - ful dance, you are our Lord, our
(my)

God. God.

Psalm 30:11a
Elise S. Eslinger

Elise S. Eslinger

I.* Lord, I exalt you, for you lift me up,
    And keep my foes from rejoicing over me
My God, I cry to you for help,
    It is you who heal me, Lord.
You brought me up from the grave;
    You restored me to life from among the dead.

II. Let faithful people sing to the Lord;
    Let them praise the holy God,
Whose anger is brief, whose grace is lifelong —
    We weep in the evening, but laugh at dawn.   ANTIPHON

I. I, unconcerned, said to myself,
    "I will never stumble."
You allowed me to stand like a splendid mountain;
    But you hid your face, and I was in terror.

II. I cried out to you, Lord;
    I sought my Lord's mercy —
"What will you gain if I die in tears?
    Does dust declare your faithful love?"

I+II. Lord, you heard, and were gracious to me;
    O Lord, you were my helper.
You turned my grief into dancing,
    Stripped me of sorrow and clothed me with joy.
So my heart will sing to you, not weep;
    Lord, my God, I will praise you forever.   ANTIPHON

Trans. Gary Chamberlain
*I and II may be read by 2 leaders; leader/congregation; male/female; 2 sides of group, etc.

92A • Psalm Prayer

Loving God, you have always been our help.
We cry to you and you hear us.
You bring healing to your people
    and deliver us from death.
Our grief you have turned to dancing
    and our sorrow to joy.
Our hearts sing to you, gracious God;
    we will praise you for ever. *Amen.*

Richard Eslinger

93 • Psalm 34
(The Cry of the Poor)

Introduction:
Capo 2: play Em

Moderate tempo ♩ = 66

REFRAIN: Congregation

The Lord hears the cry of the

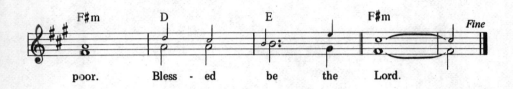

poor. Bless - ed be the Lord.

Fine

Slightly faster ♩ = 76

VERSES: Solo or choir

1. I will bless the Lord at all times, God's praise
2. Let the low - ly hear and be glad: the Lord
3. Ev - 'ry spir - it crushed God will save; will be
4. We pro - claim the great - ness of God, The Lord's praise

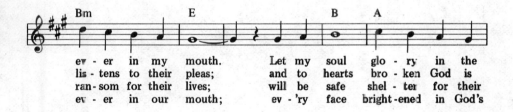

ev - er in my mouth. Let my soul glo - ry in the
lis - tens to their pleas; and to hearts bro - ken God is
ran - som for their lives; will be safe shel - ter for their
ev - er in our mouth; ev - 'ry face bright - ened in God's

Lord, for God hears the cry of the poor. The *(Refrain)*
near, for God hears the cry of the poor. The *(Refrain)*
fears, for God hears the cry of the poor. The *(Refrain)*
light, for God hears the cry of the poor. The *(Refrain)*

Psalm 34:2, 3-17; 18; 19; 23
John Foley, alt.

John Foley

93A • Psalm Prayer

In your compassion you hear the cry of the poor,
  the needy, and the lonely ones, gracious God.
May we also hear the cries of our brothers and sisters,
  responding in love as you have shown us in your Son,
  our Savior, Jesus Christ. *Amen.*

Elise S. Eslinger

94 • Psalm 51
(Create in Me a Clean Heart)

LEADER

(Am) (G6) (Am)   (Em) (D) (Em)
Cm Bb6 Cm   Gm F   Gm

Cre - ate in me a clean heart, O God,

GROUP

(Am) (G6) (F) (Em7) (Am)
Cm Bb6 Ab Gm7   Cm

And re - new a right spir - it with - in me.

LEADER

(Am) (G6) (Am)   (Em) (D) (Em)
Cm Bb6 Cm   Gm F   Gm

Cast me not a - way from Thy pres - ence,

GROUP

(Am) (G6) (F) (Em7) (Am)
Cm Bb6 Ab Gm7   Cm

And take not Thy ho - ly spir - it from me.

LEADER

(Em) (D) (Em)   (D) (Em)
Gm F   Gm   F   Gm

Re - store to me the joy of Thy sal - va - tion

GROUP

(C)   (D)   (Em)
Eb   F   Gm

And up - hold me with a will - ing spir - it.

LEADER

(Am)   (G) (Am) (Em)   (Am)
Cm   Bb Cm   Gm   Cm

Then will I teach trans - gress - ors Thy ways

Psalm 51:10-13   Jim Strathdee
Jim Strathdee

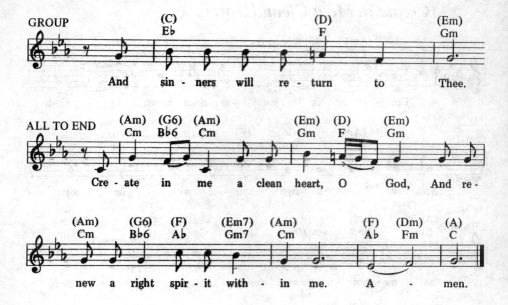

94A • Psalm Prayer

Our hearts long for your cleansing touch,
    merciful One.
Wipe away our guilt,
    renew our spirits,
        that we may serve you with joy
        all our days. *Amen.*

Elise S. Eslinger

95 • Psalm 51
(The Sacrifice You Accept)

ANTIPHON
Congregation:

The sac - ri - fice you ac - cept, O God, is a hum - ble spir - it.

VERSES
Cantor:

1. Have mercy on me, O God, in your lov - ing kindness;
2. I know full well my mis - deeds,
3. You look for truth in my in - most being,
4. Create in me a pure heart, O God,
5. Deliver me from death, O God my savior,
6. You have no delight in sacrifices
7. Glory to the Father and to the Son

in your com - passion blot out my of - fen - ses
and my sin is ever be - fore me.
and teach me wisdom in my heart.
and re - new a right spirit with - in me.
that my tongue may sing of your jus - tice.
a burnt offering from me would not please you,
and to the Holy Spir - it,

Psalm 51:1-17
Trans. Massey H. Shepherd, Jr.

David Clark Isele

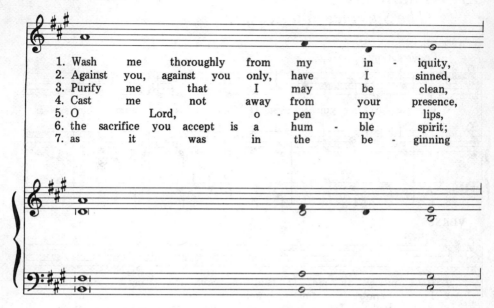

1. Wash me thoroughly from my in - iquity,
2. Against you, against you only, have I sinned,
3. Purify me that I may be clean,
4. Cast me not away from your presence,
5. O Lord, o - pen my lips,
6. the sacrifice you accept is a hum - ble spirit;
7. as it was in the be - ginning

and cleanse me from my sin.
and done what is evil in your sight.
wash me that I may be whit - er than snow.
and take not your holy Spir - it from me.
and my mouth shall pro - claim your praise.
a broken contrite heart you will not re - ject.
is now and will be for ev - er. A - men.

96 • Psalm 63
(*Longing for God in the Shadow of the Cross*)

ANTIPHON I
Congregation:

In the shad - ow of your wings I sing for joy.

or
ANTIPHON II

In the morn - ing I will sing glad songs of praise to you.

VERSES (sung, or may be read)
Leader:

1. O God, you are my God, and I long for you from ear - ly morn - ing; My whole being de - sires you; like a dry, worn - out and wa - ter - less land, my soul is thirst - y for you.
ANTIPHON

Psalm 63:1-8

Michael Joncas

4. As I lie in bed, I re-mem - ber you;

all night long I think of you, because you have al - ways been my help.

In the shadow of your wings I sing for joy. I cling to you,

and your hand keeps me safe. ANTIPHON

(optional)

5. Glo - ry to the Father, and to the Son,

and to the Ho - ly Spir - it:

as it was in the be - gin - ning, is now,

and will be forever. A - men. ANTIPHON

97 • Psalm 63
(In the Morning I Will Sing)

ANTIPHON
Congregation:

In the morn-ing I will sing glad songs of praise to you.

VERSES
Leader:

1. You are my God, I long for you from ear-ly in the morn-ing.

My whole be-ing de-sires you like a dry, worn, wa-ter-less land, My

soul thirsts for you. ANTIPHON 2. In the sanc-tu-ar-y let me

Psalm 63:1-8

David Goodrich

Music © David Goodrich 1983. Used by permission. Text adapted from *Good News Bible* © American Bible Society, 1976. Used by permission. Psalm prayer from *alive now!*, July/August 1983 © 1983 by The Upper Room.

I will sing and praise you. 4. As I lie in bed I re-
mem-ber you, O Lord; I think of you all night long, For
you are my con-stant help. In the sha-dow of your wings, I
sing for joy. I cling to you, your hand keeps me safe. ANTIPHON

97A • Psalm Prayer

We praise you with joy, loving God,
for your grace is better than life itself.
You have sustained us through the darkness;
and you bless us with life in this new day.
In the shadow of your wings we sing for joy
and bless your holy name. *Amen.*

Richard Eslinger

98 • Psalm 91
(In the Shadow of Your Wings)

ANTIPHON

Gently Congregation

In the sha-dow of your wings Lord, I cling to you

ANTIPHON

Elise S. Eslinger

I.*   You live in God's secret place;
    The Most High shades your sleep.
    You say to the Lord, "My strong refuge,
      My God, in whom I trust."

II.   God saves you from fowlers' snares,
    And from deadly disease.
    The Lord's pinions are over you;
      You hide beneath God's wings.

I.   Do not fear the terror of night,
    Or the arrow that flies by day,
    The pestilence stalking in darkness,
      The plague laying waste at noon.

II.   A thousand may fall at your side,
    Ten thousand at your right hand;
    But you will not be stricken —
      The faithful God is your shield and tower. ANTIPHON

I.   Only look with your eyes,
    And see the oppressors punished.
    As for you, the Lord is your refuge;
      You have made the Most High your shelter.

II.   Evil will not befall you,
    Nor harm approach your tent.
    On your behalf, God commanded the angels
      To guard you in all your ways.

I.   Their hands will lift you high,
    Lest you catch your foot on a stone.
    You shall step on lion and snake,
      Tread down young lion and serpent.

II.   "I will save those who cling to me,
    And protect those who know my name.
    They call and I answer them;
      I am with them in their distress.

I.+ II.   I will rescue them and reward them;
    I satisfy them with long life,
      And show them my saving power." ANTIPHON

Trans. Gary Chamberlain

*I and II may be read by two leaders: leader/people; male/female; two sides of congregation, etc.

99 • Psalm 95
(Come, Let Us Sing)

ANTIPHON

Come, let us sing to the Lord, and shout with joy to the Rock who saves us.

Psalm 95:1a
ICEL

St. Meinrad Archabbey

ANTIPHON

*Come, let us sing to the Lord;
   Let us shout to our saving rock!
Enter God's presence with praise,
   With music and shouts of joy.
For the Lord is a mighty God,
   The great ruler of all the gods.
God's hand holds the depths of the world,
   And rules the peaks of the mountains.
It is God who made and rules the seas,
   Whose hand created dry ground.
Come, let us kneel and worship the Lord;
   Let us bow before God our maker.   ANTIPHON

*May be read by one or more leaders, or antiphonally by leader and congregation.
Psalm 95:1-6
Trans. Gary Chamberlain

99A • Psalm Prayer

Our shouts of praise greet you, Shepherd God.
We have been led by your loving hand,
   and we proclaim with joy that you
   are our salvation.
Reign in our hearts this day. *Amen.*

Elise S. Eslinger

100 • Psalm 95
(To God with Gladness Sing)

1. To God with glad - ness sing, Your rock and Savior bless;
2. God cra - dles in his hand the heights and depths of earth;
3. Your heav'n - ly Fa - ther praise, Ac - claim God's on - ly Son.

With - in God's tem - ple bring your songs of thank - ful
God made the sea and land, and brought the world to
Your voice in hom - age raise to God who makes all

ness! O God of might, to you we sing
birth! O God most high, We are your sheep
one! O Dove of peace, on us de - scend,

En - throned as King on heav - en's height!
On us you keep your Shep - herd's eye!
That strife may end and joy in - crease!

Psalm 95.1-7, adapt.
James Quinn

DARWALL'S 148th
John Darwall

101 • Psalm 98
(Sing a New Song)

ANTIPHON

Sing a new song un-to the Lord;
let your song be sung from moun-tains high.
Sing a new song un-to the Lord, sing-ing al-le-lu-ia.

VERSES

1. Yah - weh's peo - ple dance for joy. O come be - fore the Lord. And play for Him on glad tam - bou - rines, and let your trum - pet sound.

2. Rise, O chil - dren, from your sleep; your Sav - ior now has come. He has turned your sor - row to joy, and filled your soul with song.

3. Glad my soul for I have seen the glo - ry of the Lord. The trum - pet sounds; the dead shall be raised. I know my Sav - ior lives.

Psalm 98, selected verses
Dan Schutte

Dan Schutte

102 • Psalm 100
(Rejoice in God, All Earthly Lands)

1. Re - joice in God, all earth - ly lands; Lift up your hearts in
2. Know this: We serve the Ho - ly One, To whom our rest - less
3. Like sheep, we wan - der with - out aim, Un - less our gen - tle
4. On God our Mak - er we de - pend For love that's gra - cious,

song and prayer. De - light to live by God's com - mands;
souls be - long. We have our breath through God a - lone,
shep - herd lead. In trust, we call up - on God's name
strong, and sure. God's faith - ful - ness shall ne - ver end;

Sing joy - ful prais - es ev - 'ry - where.
To whom we raise our grate - ful song.
For grace and hope and dai - ly bread.
From age to age it shall en - dure.

Ruth Duck

OLD 100th
Attr. Louis Bourgeois

Words by Ruth Duck, © 1981. Reprinted by her permission from *Everflowing Streams: Songs for Worship* (Pilgrim Press, 1981).

Alternate Text:

102A • WESLEY'S GRACE

Be present at our table, Lord;
Be here and everywhere adored;
Thy creatures bless, and grant that we
May feast in paradise with thee.

John Wesley

Alternate Text:

102B • DOXOLOGY

Praise God from whom
    all blessings flow;
Praise God, all creatures
    here below;
Praise God, above,
    ye heaven'ly hosts,
Praise Father, Son,
    and Holy Ghost.

Thomas Ken, alt.

103 • Psalm 100
(Cry Out with Joy)

VERSES

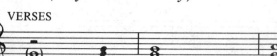

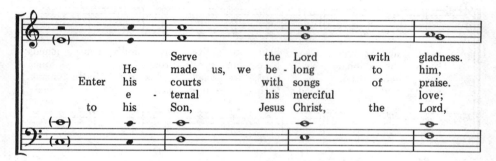

1. Cry out with joy to the Lord, all the earth.
2. Know that he, the Lord, is God.
3. Go within his gates giving thanks.
4. Indeed, how good is the Lord,
5. Give glory to the Father Almighty,

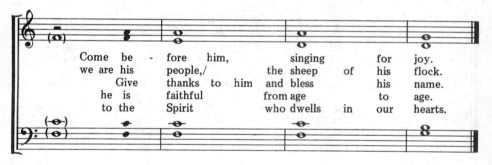

Serve the Lord with gladness.
He made us, we belong to him,
Enter his courts with songs of praise.
e - ternal his merciful love;
to his Son, Jesus Christ, the Lord,

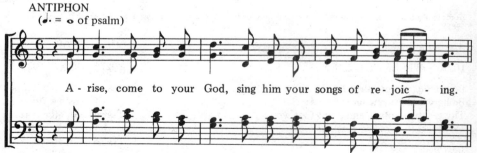

Come before him, singing for joy.
we are his people,/ the sheep of his flock.
Give thanks to him and bless his name.
he is faithful from age to age.
to the Spirit who dwells in our hearts.

ANTIPHON
(♩. = o of psalm)

A - rise, come to your God, sing him your songs of re - joic - ing.

Grail translation

Joseph Gelineau

104–I • Psalm 103
(Bless the Lord)

ANTIPHON I

Bless the Lord O my soul, who works jus-tice and vin-di-ca-tion for all who are op-pressed. Bless the Lord, O my soul.

Psalm 103:1a, 6

John S. Rice

104–II • Psalm 103
(O Bless the Lord)

ANTIPHON II* (a Round)

a) O bless the Lord, my soul, and all that is in me, bless God's ho-ly name!

b) O bless the Lord my soul, and all that is in me, bless God's ho-ly name!

*May be accompanied by hand clapping, tambourine, or other percussive instrument.

Psalm 103:1

Elise S. Eslinger

ANTIPHON

I. Bless the Lord, my inmost self!
    Everything in me, bless God's holy name.

II. Bless the Lord, my inmost self,
    Do not forget what God has done —

I. Pardoning all your sin,
    Healing your every disease,

II. Redeeming your life from the grave,
    Crowning your head with constant compassion.

I.+ II. Your vital needs are satisfied;
    Like the phoenix, your youth is renewed. ANTIPHON

I. The Lord accomplishes justice —
    Vindication for all the oppressed!

II. God's ways were made known to Moses,
    God's acts to Israel's offspring.

I. Compassion and grace — that is the Lord,
    Slow to be angry, determined to love us!

II. God will not always oppose us,
    Nor hold a grudge forever.

I.+ II. God does not act in accord with our sins,
    Nor as our guilt deserves.   ANTIPHON

I. As high as the sky is above the world,
    So great is the grace given those who fear God.

II. As far as the east is from the west,
    God removes our offences from us.

I.+ II. Like a father's love for his child
    Is the love shown to those who fear God.   ANTIPHON

Psalm 103:1-13

Trans. Gary Chamberlain

104A • Psalm Prayer

You are compassion and grace, almighty God.
We join your creatures everywhere
    in blessing your name, holy and loving One.
Glory be to the Father, Son, and Holy Spirit,
    world without end. *Amen.*

Elise S. Eslinger

105 • Psalm 118 — *Selected*
(This Is the Day)

*Parts I and II may be sung by leader/people or two groups within the congregation.

Anonymous, based on scripture   Fiji Islands Folk Melody

106–I • Psalm 121
(Our Help Comes from the Lord)

ANTIPHON 1

Our help comes from the Lord, the mak-er of heav-en and earth.

Psalm 121:2

Michael Joncas

106–II • Psalm 121
(My Help Comes from the Lord)

or
ANTIPHON 2

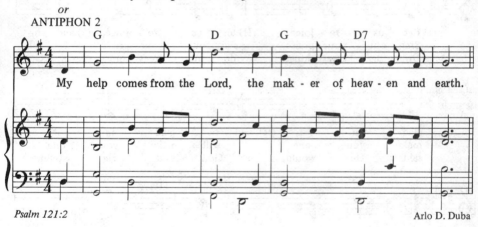

My help comes from the Lord, the mak-er of heav-en and earth.

Psalm 121:2

Arlo D. Duba

ANTIPHON

I *I look at the hills, and wonder
　From where will my help come?

II My help comes from the Lord,
　The maker of earth and sky.

I May God not let you stumble;
　May God your protector not sleep!

II Truly God never rests or sleeps,
　Protecting Israel.　　ANTIPHON

II The sun will not strike you by day,
　Nor the moon at night.

I The Lord protects you from every evil;
　God protects your life.

I The Lord is your protector,
　The shade at your right hand.

II The Lord will protect you, coming and going,
　Now, and forevermore.　　ANTIPHON

Trans. Gary Chamberlain

*I and II may be read by leader/people or two groups with the congregation.

106A • Psalm Prayer

Father of Jesus and Source of the Spirit,
we came forth from your heart
when we were born in this world.
We return to you
when we show you our love on the pilgrimage of this life.
Watch over our going and our coming to you,
through Jesus Christ, in the Spirit of love. *Amen.*

Lucien Deiss

107 • Psalm 130
(Lord, Listen to My Voice)

**OSTINATO: Choir and Congregation

Lord, lis-ten to my voice.

**To be sung continuously by choir and congregation while solo voice sings verses of the Psalm.
Instruments also may improvise occasional verses over congregation and choir.

Cantor(s): When Ostinato is established, cantor begins. *(Allow choir and congregation to sing Ostinato one or two times between verses, and at end.)

*1. From the depths I cry to you; Lord, lis-ten to my voice.

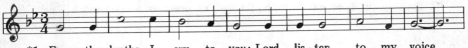

Let your ear be o-pen to the sound of my plea for par-don, (Lord.)

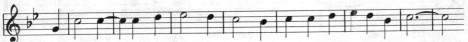

2. If* you, Lord keep ac-count of wrongs, Lord, who will be a-ble to stand?

But you are pre-pared to for-give us, so that we may wor-ship you,(Lord)

Trans. Gary Chamberlain

Taizé-style

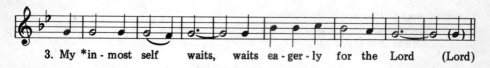

3. My *in-most self waits, waits ea-ger-ly for the Lord (Lord)

*4. I stand wait-ing, wait-ing for the Word of the Lord, (Lord.)

5. I *tell my-self, "Wait for the Lord, as a sen-try watch-es for morn-ing." (Lord.)

6. As a *sen-try watch-es for morn-ing, Is-ra-el, wait for the Lord (Lord.)

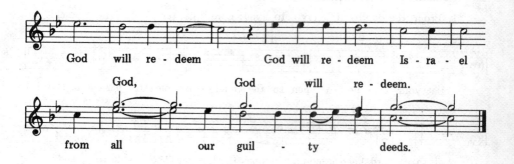

God will re-deem   God will re-deem   Is-ra-el

God,   God   will   re-deem.

from   all   our   guil-ty   deeds.

107A • Psalm Prayer

Hear our prayer, O Lord,
     and show us your salvation.
In your mercy, be near to us.
We long for you, Lord — you are our hope.
We long for you, Lord — be known to us.
We long for you, Lord — redeem us from our sin. *Amen.*

Douglas Mills

108 • Psalm 141
(My Prayers Rise Like Incense)

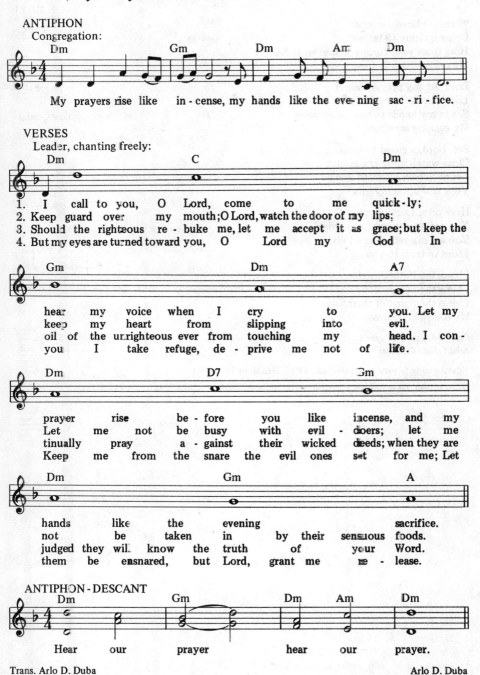

ANTIPHON
Congregation:

My prayers rise like in-cense, my hands like the eve-ning sac-ri-fice.

VERSES
Leader, chanting freely:

1. I call to you, O Lord, come to me quick-ly;
2. Keep guard over my mouth; O Lord, watch the door of my lips;
3. Should the righteous re-buke me, let me accept it as grace; but keep the
4. But my eyes are turned toward you, O Lord my God In

hear my voice when I cry to you. Let my
keep my heart from slipping into evil.
oil of the unrighteous ever from touching my head. I con-
you I take refuge, de-prive me not of life.

prayer rise be-fore you like incense, and my
Let me not be busy with evil-doers; let me
tinually pray a-gainst their wicked deeds; when they are
Keep me from the snare the evil ones set for me; Let

hands like the evening sacrifice.
not be taken in by their sensuous foods.
judged they will know the truth of your Word.
them be ensnared, but Lord, grant me re-lease.

ANTIPHON - DESCANT

Hear our prayer hear our prayer.

Trans. Arlo D. Duba

Arlo D. Duba
Descant, Elise S. Eslinger

108A • Psalm 141
(I Call, O Lord, on You)

*I call, O Lord, on you:
Come quickly to my aid,
Hear from your throne in heaven above
My cry of deep distress.

Lord, let my prayer ascend
Like incense in your sight;
See in my hands to heaven upraised
My evening sacrifice.

Set, Lord, a guard to keep
Close watch upon my mouth;
Let no rebellious word escape
Your seal upon my lips.

Have pity, Lord on me;
You are my strength, my shield:
You are my refuge in all ills;
I turn in trust to you.

I bless the Father's name;
I bless the Savior-Son;
I bless the Spirit of their love,
My solace in distress.

Psalm 141, selected verses
Adapt. James Quinn

*May be sung to tune SOUTHWELL, TRENTHAM, or ST. BRIDE.

109 • Psalm 146
(Praise to the One)

Psalm 146:7b, 8a
Elise S. Eslinger

Elise S. Eslinger

praise the God of Sha - lom!

Praise, Sha - lom.

ANTIPHON

I.   *Praise the Lord!
        My inmost self, praise the Lord,
     Praise the Lord as long as I live;
        I will constantly sing to my God.

II. Do not depend on the noblest people,
        For no human power can save you.
     Their breath departs; they return to the ground;
        On that very day their plans will perish.

I.   Happy are those whose helper is Jacob's God,
        Whose hope is in God the Lord —
     The maker of earth and sky and sea,
        And all the things that are in them;

II. Who always does what is right,
        Who brings justice to all the oppressed,
     The Lord, who gives food to the famished,
        The Lord, who sets the prisoner free,

I.   The Lord, who gives sight to the blind,
II.   The Lord, who lifts up the humbled,
I.   The Lord, who loves those who act justly,
II.   The Lord, who protects the refugees,
I.   Who comes to the aid of the orphan and widow,
II.   But subverts the plans of evil people.

ALL: The Lord will always rule,
        Your God, O Zion, forevermore.

ANTIPHON (May be sung as a round.)

Trans. Gary Chamberlain

*I and II may be read by leader/people or by two groups within the congregation.

110 • Psalm 150
(Let All Who Breathe)

ANTIPHON

Let all who breathe praise the Lord. Let Lord.

a Praise God in the earth - ly tem - ple; b Praise God in heav-en's great dome.

a Praise God the might - y hero; b Praise God, su-preme-ly great. ANTIPHON

a Praise God with blast - ing trum-pets; b Praise God with harps and lyres.

Trans. Gary Chamberlain   David Goodrich

Antiphon and verse from *Psalms for Singing,* translation of Psalms by Gary Chamberlain, © 1984 by The Upper Room. Music © David Goodrich, 1984. Psalm prayer from *Come, Lord Jesus,* © Copyright 1976, 1981, Lucien Deiss, published by World Library Publications, Inc. Used by permission.

a Praise God with drums and danc-ing; b Praise God with strings and flutes. ANTIPHON

a Praise God with sound-ing cym-bals; ɔ Praise God with clam-orous joy.

a Let all who breathe, praise the Lord. b Praise the Lord, Halle-lu-jah! ANTIPHON

110A • Psalm Prayer

Blessed are you, Father of Jesus and Source of the Spirit!

All beauty is a spark of the fire of your splendor,
all music is an echo of your harmony,
all kindness is a fragment of your excellence,
all creatures praise your love!

May you be blessed, Father,
by the dew of the morning and the damp fragrance of the evening,
by the song of the nightingale and the perfume of the rose,
by the smile of our children and the grace of our girls,
by the daring of youth and the wisdom of elders,
by the love of the husband and the tenderness of the wife,
by the peace of the pardoned sinner,
and by the holiness of the people in the street!

Blessed are you, expecially blessed,
by the humble and poor heart
that trembles with love for you!

May every creature that has breath sing your praise.
May every instant of our life shout "Alleluia" to your glory!

Through Christ, in him, with him,
in the unity of the Holy Spirit,
all glory and honor is yours, Almighty Father,
forever and ever! *Amen.*

Lucien Deiss

111 • Psalm 150
(Praise Ye the Lord)

Psalm 150:1-5
J. Jefferson Cleveland

CANTOR'S MELODY (VERSE)

1. Praise God with the sound of the trum - pet,
2. Praise God with ho - ly cym - bals,
3. Praise God in the ho - ly ple,
4. Praise God on top of the moun - tains,

Praise God with the lute and the harp;
Praise God with strings and with pipes;
Praise God for al - might - y deeds;
Praise God both day and night;

Praise God with tim - brel and danc - ing,
Praise God with clash - ing cym - bals,
Praise God for those boun - ti - ful mer - cies,
Praise God down in the low val - leys,

Praise God wher - ev - er you are.
Praise God with all of your might.
For God ful - fills our needs.
Praise God be - cause it's al - right.

V

LITURGIES FOR DAILY PRAYER AND CANTICLES

Included in this section are basic patterns for daily prayer which may be elaborated or made more sparse. The rhythms of morning and evening, the emotive content of the Psalms, and the prayerful attitude of the worshiper provide an environment for listening to the word and the Spirit. The patterns of prayer are quiet and gently paced in order to offer the community space for silence and reflection as well as for vocal prayer and song.

The pattern is as follows for both morning and evening prayer:

> Opening (Greeting, Hymn, and Prayer)
> Psalmody
> Scripture Reading
> Canticle or Song
> Prayers of Thanksgiving, Intercession
> Canticle or Song
> Dismissal

The pattern for Night Prayer is similar but calls for an "end of day" self-examination and confession. At all the prayer services, the thanksgivings and intercessions may be free or guided, offered for the world, the church, the community, neighbors near and far, and ourselves.

The Psalms are at the heart of daily prayer; discussion of their use may be found in Section IV of the *Worshipbook*. The reading from scripture is usually brief (many persons follow a daily lectionary of readings) and may be followed by a time for meditation and silent prayer. The traditional canticles assigned to morning (Song of Mary, the *Magnificat*), to evening (Song of Zechariah, the *Benedictus*), and to Night Prayer (Song of Simeon, the *Nunc Dimittis*) may be interchanged, or other songs of praise may be substituted. The three canticles* included in several settings at the end of each service provide rich continuity with Old Testament story and prophecy, emerging as New Testament "psalms."

Leadership for the prayer services may be provided by lay persons, who may appropriately serve as liturgists, since neither preaching nor the sacraments are generally involved. The basic patterns of daily prayer should be internalized when possible. Whenever the pattern requires less conscious attention, then inner and outer environment may truly become listening space, breathing space, for the Spirit and our own spirits. Long tradition has affirmed daily prayer patterns as spiritually formative by simplicity, repetition, and provision of opportunity for disciplined attentiveness to the word. Join the saints through the ages and all creation; let all that has breath praise the Lord!

*Other canticles of praise may be chosen from the following: Song of Moses (Exod. 15:1–6, 11–13, 17–18); First Song of Isaiah (Isa. 12:2–6); Second Song of Isaiah (Isa. 55:6–11); Third Song of Isaiah (Isa. 60:1–3, 11, 14, 18–19); A Song to the Lamb (Rev. 4:11; 5:9–10, 13); The Song of the Redeemed (Rev. 15:3–4); Gloria in Excelsis; Te Deum Laudamus.

112 • A Liturgy for Morning Prayer

OPENING

(Liturgist)   (People)

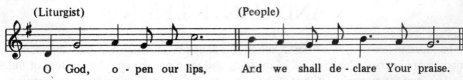

O God, o-pen our lips, And we shall de-clare Your praise.

Psalm 51:15   Elise S. Eslinger

OR

God said: Let there be light; and there was light.
And God saw that the light was good. This very day
the Lord has acted!
LET US REJOICE!
Praise the Lord!
GOD'S NAME BE PRAISED!

Morning Hymn or *Psalm 95* (May be selected from Section I, Nos. 18-27.)

Prayer

New every morning is your love, great God of light, and all day long you
are working for good in the world. Stir up in us desire to serve you, to
live peacefully with our neighbors, and to devote each day to your Son,
our Savior, Jesus Christ the Lord. AMEN. [1]

PSALMODY (See Section IV.)

Psalm 63 (sung or read)

Silence

Psalm Prayer

Let us pray together.
WE PRAISE YOU WITH JOY, LOVING GOD,
    FOR YOUR GRACE IS BETTER THAN LIFE ITSELF.
YOU HAVE SUSTAINED US THROUGH THE DARKNESS:
    AND YOU BLESS US WITH LIFE IN THIS NEW DAY.
IN THE SHADOW OF YOUR WINGS WE SING FOR JOY
    AND BLESS YOUR HOLY NAME. AMEN. [2]

(Other Psalms may be sung or said.)

READING FROM SCRIPTURE

(After the reading)

This is the Word of the Lord!
THANKS BE TO GOD.

(Silence for reflection and prayer or other group response to the
Word may follow.)

CANTICLE OF ZACHARY ("Benedictus")   Luke 1:68-79
        (A setting may be chosen from Nos. 113-113D.)

                        OR

HYMN OF PRAISE

PRAYERS OF THANKSGIVING, INTERCESSION, PETITION

        In peace, let us pray to the Lord.
        LORD, HAVE MERCY.

        (Here may follow prayers of thanksgiving and prayers for the world,
        the Church, for family and friends, for the community.)

THE LORD'S PRAYER (Said or sung, see No. 122.)

        OUR FATHER IN HEAVEN,
            HALLOWED BE YOUR NAME,
            YOUR KINGDOM COME,
            YOUR WILL BE DONE,
                ON EARTH AS IN HEAVEN.
        GIVE US TODAY OUR DAILY BREAD.
        FORGIVE US OUR SINS
            AS WE FORGIVE THOSE
                WHO SIN AGAINST US.
        SAVE US FROM THE TIME OF TRIAL,
            AND DELIVER US FROM EVIL.
        FOR THE KINGDOM, THE POWER, AND THE GLORY
            ARE YOURS
                NOW AND FOR EVER.
        AMEN. [3]

HYMN OR DOXOLOGY

BENEDICTION

        Go in peace. Serve the Lord. The grace of our Lord Jesus Christ be
        with you all. AMEN. [4]

SHARING OF THE PEACE

                    * * * * * * * * *

113 • Benedictus—Canticle of Zachary *(TEXT)*

*Blessed be the Lord, the God of Israel;
he has come to his people and set them free.
He has raised up for us a mighty savior,
born of the house of his servant David.
Through his holy prophets he promised of old
    that he would save us from our enemies,
    from the hands of all who hate us.

He promised to show mercy to our fathers
and to remember his holy covenant.
This was the oath he swore to our father Abraham:
to set us free from the hands of our enemies,
free to worship him without fear,
holy and righteous in his sight all the days of our life.

You, my child, shall be called the prophet of the Most High,
for you will go before the Lord to prepare his way
to give his people knowledge of salvation
by the forgiveness of their sins.
In the tender compassion of our God
the dawn from on high shall break upon us,
to shine on those who dwell in darkness
    and the shadow of death,
and to guide our feet into the way of peace.

Luke 1:68-79
*Verses may be read in unison, or alternately by leader/congregation, choir/congregation, men/women,
right/left, etc. Verses may also be chanted on a single tone (pitch) or according to improvised patterns.

From *Prayers We Have in Common,* 2nd revised ed., 1975. Used by permission of ICET.

113A • Benedictus–Canticle of Zachary
(Blessed Be the God of Israel)

1. Blessed be the God of Is - rael, who comes to set us free, who
2. Now from the house of Da - vid a child of grace is giv'n; a
3. Where once were fear and dark - ness the sun be - gins to rise — the

vis - its and re - deems us, and grants us lib - er - ty. The
Sav - ior comes a - mong us to raise us up to heaven. Be -
dawn - ing of for - give - ness up - on the sin - ner's eyes, to

proph - ets spoke of mer - cy, of free - dom and re - lease; God
fore him goes the her - ald—fore - run - ner in the way — the
guide the feet of pil - grims a - long the paths of peace: O

shall ful - fill the prom - ise to bring our peo - ple peace.
pro - phet of sal - va - tion, the har - bin - ger of Day.
bless our God and Sav - ior, with songs that nev - er cease!

Luke 1:68-79
Metrical Benedictus
Michael A. Perry (b. 1942)

MERLE'S TUNE
Hal H. Hopson

113B • Benedictus—Canticle of Zachary
(Bless'd Be the God of Israel)

Capo 5

1. Bless'd be the God of Is-ra-el, The ev-er liv-ing Lord,
2. Through ho-ly pro-phets did he speak His word in days of old,
3. Of old he gave his sol-emn oath To Fa-ther A-bra-ham;
4. O ti-ny child, your name shall be The pro-phet of the Lord;
5. The ris-ing sun shall shine on us To bring the light of day

1. Who comes in pow'r to save his own, His peo-ple Is-ra-el.
2. That he would save us from our foes And all who bear us ill.
3. His seed a might-y race should be And bless'd for-ev-er-more.
4. The way of God you shall pre-pare To make his com-ing known.
5. To all who sit in dark-est night And sha-dow of the grave.

1. For Is-ra-el he rai-ses up, Sal-va-tion's tow'r on high
2. To our an-ces-tors did he give His co-ve-nant of love
3. He vowed to set his peo-ple free From fear of ev-'ry foe
4. You shall pro-claim to Is-ra-el Sal-va-tion's dawn-ing day
5. Our foot-steps God shall safe-ly guide To walk the ways of peace.

Luke 1:68-79

Trans. James Quinn, S.J.

FOREST GREEN
Coll., adapt. and arr. Ralph Vaughan Williams (1872-1958)
Guitar chords, Michael Joncas

*N. B. The guitar chords and written harmonization are not compatible.

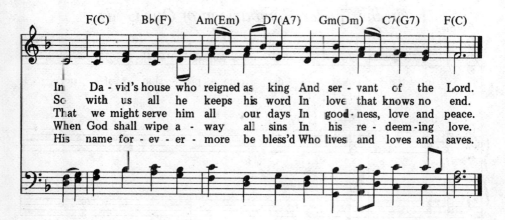

In Da - vid's house who reigned as king And ser - vant of the Lord.
So with us all he keeps his word In love that knows no end.
That we might serve him all our days In good - ness, love and peace.
When God shall wipe a - way all sins In his re - deem - ing love.
His name for - ev - er - more be bless'd Who lives and loves and saves.

113C • Benedictus–Canticle of Zachary
(In the Tender Compassion of Our God)

In the ten- der com- pas- sion of our God the morn- ing sun from heav- en will rise___ up- on us, to shine on those who live in

* Accompaniment is a "clue" to chordal structure — improvised eighths, arpeggio-style, are encouraged.

Luke 1:78-79

Elise S. Eslinger

114 • A Liturgy for Evening Prayer

(Choose Opening A or B.)

A. OPENING SERVICE OF LIGHT

Light Proclamation (Vesper candle is lit)

(Liturgist)   (People)

Light and peace in Je-sus Christ, our Lord. THANKS BE TO GOD.

Evening Hymn
*ANTIPHON (Sung at beginning and end)

Je-sus Christ is the light of the world.

1. O gracious Light, pure brightness of the everliving Father in heaven.

O Je-sus Christ Holy and blessed!

2. Now as we come to the setting of the sun And our eyes behold the Vesper Light,

We sing Your praises O God: Father, Son, and Ho-ly Spirit.

3. You are worthy at all times to be praised by hap-py voices,

O Son of God, O giver of life, and to be glorified through all the worlds. ANTIPHON

*Accompaniment at end of order.

PHOS HILERON, 4th Century Greek Hymn   Mode 8
Trans. BOOK OF COMMON PRAYER   St. Meinrad Archabbey

Music for verses © 1984. Prepared by the Benedictine Monks, St. Meinrad Archabbey, St. Meinrad, Indiana 47577 USA.
Antiphon © 1985 by The Upper Room.

OR

B. OPENING

From the rising of the sun to its setting,
Let the name of the Lord be praised.
YOU, O LORD, ARE MY LAMP.
MY GOD, YOU MAKE MY DARKNESS BRIGHT.
Light and peace in Jesus Christ our Lord.
THANKS BE TO GOD.

EVENING HYMN (May be selected from Section I, Nos. 18-27.)

(This may be a processional hymn with the vesper candle when the opening service of light is not used.)

PRAYER

We praise and thank you, O God,
  for you are without beginning and without end.
Through Christ, you created the whole world;
  through Christ, you preserve it.
You made the day for the works of light
  and the night for the refreshment of our minds and our bodies.
Keep us now in Christ, grant us a peaceful evening,
  a night free from sin, and bring us at last to eternal life.
Through Christ and in the Holy Spirit,
  we offer you all glory, honor and worship,
  now and for ever. AMEN.

PSALMODY

Psalm(s)

(Psalm 141, 121, or other Psalms may be sung or read. These may be chosen from Section IV.)

Silence

Psalm Prayer

SOVEREIGN GOD, YOU HAVE BEEN OUR HELP DURING
THE DAY AND YOU PROMISE TO BE WITH US AT NIGHT.
RECEIVE THIS PRAYER AS A SIGN OF OUR TRUST IN YOU.
SAVE US FROM ALL EVIL, KEEP US FROM ALL HARM, AND
GUIDE US IN YOUR WAY. WE BELONG TO YOU, LORD.
PROTECT US BY THE POWER OF YOUR NAME, IN JESUS
CHRIST, WE PRAY. AMEN. [1]

READING OF SCRIPTURE

(Following the Scripture, the reader may say:)

This is the Word of the Lord.
THANKS BE TO GOD.

(Silence for reflection, a brief homily, or group response to the
Word may follow.)

CANTICLE OF MARY ("Magnificat")   Luke 1:46-55

(A setting may be chosen from Nos. 115-115D.)

PRAYERS OF INTERCESSION (The following or other)**

In peace, let us pray to the Lord.
LORD, HAVE MERCY.

For the peace of the world, that a spirit of respect and forbearance may grow among nations and peoples, let us pray to the Lord. LORD, HAVE MERCY.

For the holy church of God, that it may be filled with truth and love, and be found without fault at the day of your coming, let us pray to the Lord. LORD, HAVE MERCY.

For those in positions of public trust, (especially_____), that they may serve justice and promote the dignity and freedom of all people, let us pray to the Lord. LORD, HAVE MERCY.

For a blessing upon the labors of all, and for the right use of the riches of creation, let us pray to the Lord. LORD, HAVE MERCY.

For the poor, the persecuted, the sick, and all who suffer; for refugees, prisoners and all who are in danger: that they may be relieved and protected, let us pray to the Lord. LORD, HAVE MERCY.

For this community; for those who are present, and for those who are absent, that we may be delivered from hardness of heart, and may show forth your glory in all that we do, we pray to the Lord. LORD, HAVE MERCY.

For our enemies and those who wish us harm; and for all whom we have injured or offended, let us pray to the Lord. LORD, HAVE MERCY.

For ourselves; for the forgiveness of our sins, and for the grace of the Holy Spirit to amend our lives, let us pray to the Lord. LORD, HAVE MERCY.

For all who commended themselves to our prayers: for our families, friends and neighbors; that being freed from anxiety, they may live in joy, peace and health, let us pray to the Lord. LORD, HAVE MERCY.

For all who have died in the faith of Christ, that with all the saints, they may have rest in that place where there is no pain or grief, but life eternal, let us pray to the Lord. LORD, HAVE MERCY.

Help, save, pity and defend us, O God, by your grace.

(Pause for silent prayer. Other petitions may be spoken by members of the community.)

In the communion of the Holy Spirit and of all the saints, let us commend ourselves and one another to the living God through Christ our Lord. AMEN. [2]

**May be sung:

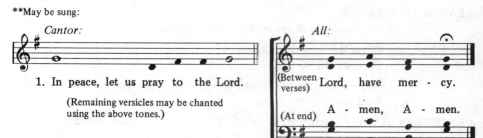

1. In peace, let us pray to the Lord.

(Remaining versicles may be chanted using the above tones.)

(Between verses) Lord, have mer - cy.

(At end) A - men, A - men.

THE LORD'S PRAYER (May be sung; see No. 122.)

> OUR FATHER IN HEAVEN,
>   HALLOWED BE YOUR NAME,
>   YOUR KINGDOM COME,
>   YOUR WILL BE DONE,
>   ON EARTH AS IN HEAVEN.
> GIVE US TODAY OUR DAILY BREAD.
> FORGIVE US OUR SINS
>   AS WE FORGIVE THOSE
>   WHO SIN AGAINST US.
> SAVE US FROM THE TIME OF TRIAL
>   AND DELIVER US FROM EVIL.
> FOR THE KINGDOM, THE POWER, AND THE GLORY
>   ARE YOURS
>   NOW AND FOR EVER.
> AMEN. [3]

EVENING HYMN OR DOXOLOGY

OR

CANTICLE OF SIMEON ("Nunc Dimittis")   Luke 2:29-32
                    (See Nos. 117-117C.)

BENEDICTION

> Eternal Creator of light,
> Yours is the morning
>   and yours is the evening.
> Draw us to yourself
>   so there will be no darkness
>   within us.
> AMEN.
> Let us go in peace.
> THANKS BE TO GOD. [4]

SHARING OF THE PEACE

* * * * * * * * * *

Alternate settings of "Phos Hileron," evening hymns, Psalm settings, and canticles may
  be found in other sections of the Worshipbook.

1. From *alive now!* July/August 1983. ©1983 by The Upper Room.
2. From *The Book of Common Prayer*, © The Church Pension Fund. Used by permission.
3. From *Prayers We Have in Common*, 2nd revised ed., 1975. Used by permission of ICET.
4. From *alive now!* July/August 1983. © 1983 by The Upper Room.

ANTIPHON (Sung before verse 1 and after verse 3.)

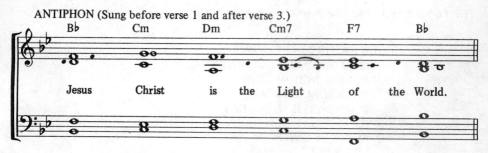

Jesus   Christ   is   the   Light   of   the   World.

Elise S. Eslinger

*Accompaniment to "Phos Hileron"

VERSES (1-3)

Mode 8
St. Meinrad Archabbey

115 • Magnificat–Canticle of Mary (TEXT)

My soul proclaims the greatness of the Lord,
   my spirit rejoices in God my Savior;
   for he has looked with favor on his lowly servant.
From this day all generations will call me blessed:
   the Almighty has done great things for me,
   and holy is his Name.
*He has mercy on those who fear him
   in every generation.
He has shown the strength of his arm,
   he has scattered the proud in their conceit.
He has cast down the mighty from their thrones,
   and has lifted up the lowly.
He has filled the hungry with good things,
   and the rich he has sent away empty.
He has come to the help of his servant Israel
   for he has remembered his promise of mercy,
The promise he made to our fathers,
   to Abraham and his children for ever.

*Editor's note: Users may wish to substitute "God" or "The Holy One" for the masculine pronoun.

Luke 1:46-55
ICET

From *Prayers We Have in Common*, 2nd revised ed., 1975. Used by permission of ICET.

115A • Magnificat–Canticle of Mary
(My Soul Gives Glory to the Lord)

Alternate Text

1. My soul gives glory to the Lord, My heart pours out its praise.
   God lifted up my lowliness in many marvelous ways.
   God lifted up my lowliness in many marvelous ways.

2. The Lord has done great things for me: Holy is this Name.
   All people will declare me blessed, and blessings they shall claim.
   All people will declare me blessed, and blessings they shall claim.

3. From age to age, to all who fear, such mercy Love imparts,
   dispensing justice far and near, dismissing selfish hearts.
   dispensing justice far and near, dismissing selfish hearts.

4. Love* casts the mighty from their thrones, promotes the insecure,
   leaves hungry spirits satisfied, the rich seem suddenly poor.
   leaves hungry spirits satisfied, the rich seem suddenly poor.

5. The Lord is true to Israel, alert to ev'ry need,
   remembering past promises to Abraham and his seed.
   Remembering past promises to Abraham and his seed.

6. (Repeat verse 1.)

*Editor's note: "God" may be substituted for "Love."

Luke 1:46-55
Miriam Therese Winter

Tune: MORNING SONG
(See No. 20.)

Copyright © 1978 by Medical Mission Sisters, Phil., Pa. Used by permission.

115B • Magnificat–Canticle of Mary
(My Soul Proclaims the Greatness of the Lord)

*ANTIPHON:

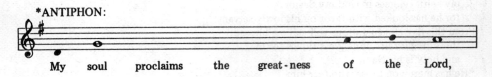

My soul proclaims the great-ness of the Lord,

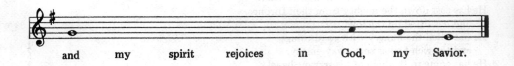

and my spirit rejoices in God, my Savior.

VERSES:

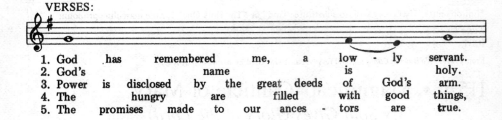

1. God has remembered me, a low - ly servant.
2. God's name is holy.
3. Power is disclosed by the great deeds of God's arm.
4. The hungry are filled with good things,
5. The promises made to our ances - tors are true.

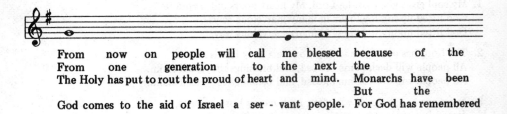

From now on people will call me blessed because of the
From one generation to the next the
The Holy has put to rout the proud of heart and mind. Monarchs have been
But the
God comes to the aid of Israel a ser - vant people. For God has remembered

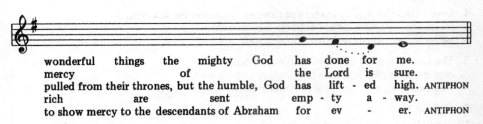

wonderful things the mighty God has done for me.
mercy of the Lord is sure.
pulled from their thrones, but the humble, God has lift - ed high. ANTIPHON
rich are sent emp - ty a - way.
to show mercy to the descendants of Abraham for ev - er. ANTIPHON

*Accompaniment follows.
Luke 1:46-55
Paraphrased by Diedra Kriewald

Elise S. Eslinger

Optional Accompaniment:

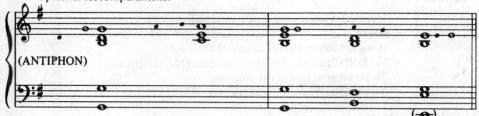

(ANTIPHON)

(VERSES)

Optional Handbells:

(May be used to introduce antiphon, and at end.)

116 • A Liturgy for Night Prayer

OPENING

> May God Almighty grant us a quiet night and peace at the last.
> AMEN.
> It is good to give thanks to you, O God,
> TO SING PRAISES TO YOUR NAME, O MOST HIGH;
> To herald your love in the morning,
> YOUR TRUTH AT THE CLOSE OF THE DAY. [1]

EVENING HYMN (May be chosen from Section I.)

CONFESSION

> Let us confess our sins in the presence of God and one another.
> (Silence for self-examination and confession.)

> Let us pray.
> HOLY AND GRACIOUS GOD, I CONFESS THAT I HAVE SINNED
> AGAINST YOU THIS DAY. SOME OF MY SIN I KNOW − −
> THE THOUGHTS AND WORDS AND DEEDS OF WHICH I AM
> ASHAMED − − BUT SOME IS KNOWN ONLY TO YOU.
> IN THE NAME OF JESUS CHRIST, I ASK FORGIVENESS.
> DELIVER AND RESTORE ME, THAT I MAY REST IN PEACE.

> By the mercy of God we are united with Jesus Christ, and in Christ
> we are forgiven. We rest now in peace and rise in the morning to
> serve the Lord.

PSALMODY (May be chosen from Section IV.)

> *Psalm*

> *Silence*

> *Psalm Prayer*

READING FROM SCRIPTURE

> (After the reading)

> This is the Word of the Lord.
> THANKS BE TO GOD.

RESPONSE

> You have redeemed me, O Lord, God of truth.
> HEAR MY PRAYER, O LORD; LISTEN TO MY CRY.
> Keep me as the apple of your eye;
> HIDE ME IN THE SHADOW OF YOUR WINGS.
> In righteousness I shall see you;
> WHEN I AWAKE, YOUR PRESENCE WILL GIVE ME JOY.
> INTO YOUR HANDS, O LORD I COMMIT MY SPIRIT. [2]

PRAYERS

THE LORD'S PRAYER

OUR FATHER IN HEAVEN,
   HALLOWED BE YOUR NAME,
   YOUR KINGDOM COME,
   YOUR WILL BE DONE,
      ON EARTH AS IN HEAVEN.
GIVE US TODAY OUR DAILY BREAD.
FORGIVE US OUR SINS
   AS WE FORGIVE THOSE
      WHO SIN AGAINST US.
SAVE US FROM THE TIME OF TRIAL
   AND DELIVER US FROM EVIL.
FOR THE KINGDOM, THE POWER, AND THE GLORY
   ARE YOURS,
      NOW AND FOR EVER.
AMEN. [3]

CANTICLE OF SIMEON (Nunc Dimittis)   Luke 2:29-32

(May be sung or spoken. See Nos. 117A-C.)

LORD, YOU NOW HAVE SET YOUR SERVANT FREE
TO GO IN PEACE AS YOU HAVE PROMISED;
FOR THESE EYES OF MINE HAVE SEEN THE SAVIOR,
WHOM YOU HAVE PREPARED FOR ALL THE WORLD TO SEE:
A LIGHT TO ENLIGHTEN THE NATIONS,
AND THE GLORY OF YOUR PEOPLE ISRAEL.

DISMISSAL AND BLESSING

Guide us waking, O God, and guard us sleeping; that awake we
may watch with Christ, and asleep we may rest in peace.

Let us bless the Lord.
THANKS BE TO GOD.
The almighty and merciful God bless us and keep us.
AMEN.

(Depart in silence)

* * * * * * * * *

1.-2. Opening and response adapted from Prayer at the Close of the Day (Compline) from LUTHERAN BOOK OF WORSHIP, copyright 1978, by permission of Augsburg Publishing House.

3. From Prayers We Have in Common, 2nd revised ed., 1975. Used by permission of ICET.

117 • Nunc Dimittis—Canticle of Simeon *(TEXT)*

Lord, now you let your servant go in peace;
your word has been fulfilled:
my own eyes have seen the salvation
which you have prepared in the sight of every people:
a light to reveal you to the nations
and the glory of your people Israel.

Luke 2:29-32
From *Prayers We Have in Common*, 2nd revised ed., 1975. Used by permission of ICET.

117A • Nunc Dimittis—Canticle of Simeon

Alternate Text

1. My master, see, the time has come To give your servant leave,
   To go in peace, long waited for Your promise now fulfilled.
   To go in peace, long waited for Your promise now fulfilled.

2. For I have seen salvation, Lord And this may all men see:
   That light which is your Israel's boast Enlight'ning ev'ry land.
   That light which is your Israel's boast Enlight'ning ev'ry land.

3. Almighty Father, hear our cry Through Christ the only Son,
   Whom in the Spirit we adore For ages without end.
   Whom in the Spirit we adore For ages without end.

Luke 2:29-32
Frank C. Quinn

MORNING SONG
(See No. 20.)

The Grail, England. Used by permission.

117B • Nunc Dimittis–Canticle of Simeon
(Now, Lord, You Have Kept Your Word)

Luke 2:29-32

Hal H. Hopson

117C • Nunc Dimittis—Canticle of Simeon

(with Gloria Deo)
(Lord Now You Let Your Servant Go in Peace)

Lord now you let your ser - vant go in peace; your word has been ful - filled: My own eyes have seen the sal - vation which you have pre - pared in the sight of ev - ery peo - ple: A light to re -

Luke 2:29-32

James A. Kriewald

veal you to the na - tions And the Glory of your people Is - ra - el.

build
Glo - ry to God in Christ and in the ho - ly spir - it

As it was in the beginning is Now and will be for - ev - er A - men.

A - men. A - men.

VI

A LITURGY FOR HOLY COMMUNION AND SERVICE MUSIC

Somewhat in contrast to the quieter, more reflective daily prayer liturgies, the eucharistic service—a service of word and table—is a time for celebration of the word, with appropriate acts and responses, and a time to recall the mighty acts of God in salvation, always with thanksgiving, through Holy Communion (the Eucharist).

The music called for in the liturgy, as in the Sunday service, is active in its response and purpose. Through bread and wine we are connected as the Body of Christ with the reality of Christ's presence, with the communion of saints through history, with all those worldwide who gather at the Lord's table, and with a world of persons hungry for righteousness, justice, and bread. Our hymns and songs reflect thanksgiving for what God has done, is doing, and will do in Jesus Christ!

While somber silence during the sharing of bread and cup may be desirable during seasons or times of penitence, the prevailing atmosphere of this liturgy is that of praise and thanksgiving. We come to a feast of joy, not to a memorial service for a departed one. Our emphasis is on reconciled community rather than on individual unworthiness. God has redeemed us through Jesus Christ. We are forgiven! Our music, then, needs to punctuate and undergird this celebration. Hymns and songs for this specific purpose are identified in Section I of the *Worshipbook*.

Included is one musical setting within the liturgy, with several alternatives following which may be substituted as desired. In ongoing communities, through teaching and repetition, it is hoped that these responsive parts of the liturgy will soon be memorized and sung naturally and spontaneously by the congregation. The shuffle of papers and unnecessary instructions are to be avoided during the gathering at the table. In addition to hymns and songs in this resource, you may want to utilize those very familiar spirituals and hymns which can be sung without the distraction of attempting to read less familiar words and music. Singing during the offering of bread and wine and the sharing of bread and cup almost always will enhance the celebration, though thankful silence is also appropriate.

While not included as normative in this liturgy, leaders of worship will want to be aware of the possibilities for the sacrament of baptism, baptismal renewal, prayers and services of healing, footwashing, and other specific acts of response to the word of the day, the season, the themes of the occasion, the needs of the people gathered—and most of all, to the Spirit.

May our tongues sing the Redeemer's praise with renewed joy at the Lord's own table!

118 • A Service of Word and Table
(Holy Communion)

THE ENTRANCE

GATHERING

(An instrumental prelude, songs of praise, or silence for prayer may be offered.)

GREETING

The grace of the Lord Jesus Christ be with you.
AND ALSO WITH YOU.
The risen Christ is with us.
PRAISE THE LORD!

HYMN OF PRAISE

OPENING PRAYER

(The following or a prayer of the day is offered.)
ALMIGHTY GOD, TO YOU ALL HEARTS ARE OPEN, ALL DESIRES
KNOWN, AND FROM YOU NO SECRETS ARE HIDDEN. CLEANSE
THE THOUGHTS OF OUR HEARTS BY THE INSPIRATION OF YOUR
HOLY SPIRIT, THAT WE MAY PERFECTLY LOVE YOU, AND
WORTHILY MAGNIFY YOUR HOLY NAME, THROUGH CHRIST OUR
LORD. AMEN.

ACT OF PRAISE*

PROCLAMATION AND RESPONSE

PRAYER FOR ILLUMINATION

LORD, OPEN OUR HEARTS AND MINDS BY THE POWER OF YOUR
HOLY SPIRIT, THAT, AS THE SCRIPTURES ARE READ AND YOUR
WORD PROCLAIMED, WE MAY HEAR WITH JOY WHAT YOU SAY TO
US TODAY. AMEN.

SCRIPTURE LESSON*

PSALM*

SCRIPTURE LESSON*

HYMN, SONG, OR ANTHEM*

GOSPEL LESSON

SERMON OR HOMILY

RESPONSE TO THE WORD*

(May include a hymn, psalm, or song, acts of renewal and commitment.)

CONCERNS AND PRAYERS*

(Intercessions and petitions may be prayed by the people, or a pastoral prayer offered.)

---

*May be omitted when a shorter service is necessary.

This service has been adapted from *A Service of Word and Table, Complete Text, 1984 Edition.* Copyright © 1972, 1976, 1979, 1980, and 1984 by The United Methodist Publishing House. Used by permission. The musical settings in this service were written by Elise S. Eslinger, © 1985 by The Upper Room. The texts for the Sanctus and Benedictus and The Lord's Prayer are from *Prayers We Have in Common*, 2nd revised ed., 1975. Used by permission.

Accompaniment for the musical settings may be found at the end of the service, No. 118a-c. For alternate settings, see Nos. 119, 120, and 121. For musical settings for The Lord's Prayer, see Nos. 122A-E.

CONFESSION AND PARDON

Christ our Lord invites to his table all who love him, who earnestly repent of their sin and seek to live in peace with one another. Therefore, let us confess our sin before God and one another.

WE DO NOT PRESUME TO COME TO THIS YOUR TABLE, MERCIFUL LORD, TRUSTING IN OUR OWN GOODNESS, BUT IN YOUR UNFAILING MERCY. WE ARE NOT WORTHY TO RECEIVE YOU, BUT ONLY SAY THE WORD AND WE SHALL BE HEALED.

(All pray in silence.)

Hear the good news:
"Christ died for us while we were yet sinners: that proves God's love toward us." In the name of Jesus Christ, you are forgiven!

IN THE NAME OF JESUS CHRIST, YOU ARE FORGIVEN!

(Minister and people)
GLORY TO GOD. AMEN.

THE PEACE

Let us offer one another signs of reconciliation and love.
(All may exchange signs or words of God's peace, e.g., "The peace of Christ be with you.")

OFFERING

As forgiven and reconciled people, let us offer ourselves and our gifts to God.
(A hymn, psalm, or anthem may be sung as the offering of money or other gifts, and the bread and wine are brought to the Lord's table.)

THANKSGIVING AND COMMUNION

TAKING THE BREAD AND CUP

(The minister receives the bread and wine, and the table is prepared.)

THE GREAT THANKSGIVING (The people standing.)

The Lord be with you.
AND ALSO WITH YOU.
Lift up your hearts.
WE LIFT THEM TO THE LORD.
Let us give thanks to the Lord our God.
IT IS RIGHT TO GIVE OUR THANKS AND PRAISE.

It is right, and a good and joyful thing,
always and everywhere to give thanks to you,
Father almighty, creator of heaven and earth.
You formed us in your own image and breathed
into us the breath of life.
When we turned away, and our love failed, your love
remained steadfast. You delivered us from captivity,
made covenant to be our sovereign God, and spoke to us
through your prophets.
And so, with your people on earth and all the company
of heaven we praise your name and join their unending hymn:

a. Sanctus and Benedictus (Sung or read by the people.)

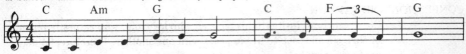

HO - LY, HO - LY, HO - LY LORD, GOD OF POW-ER AND MIGHT,

HEAV-EN AND EARTH ARE FULL OF YOUR GLO-RY. HO - SAN-NA IN THE

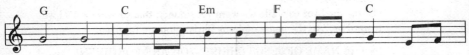

HIGH - EST. BLESS-ED IS HE WHO COMES IN THE NAME OF THE

LORD. HO - SAN - NA IN THE HIGH - EST!

Holy are you, and blessed is your Son Jesus Christ.

Your Spirit anointed him to preach good news to the poor, to proclaim release to the captives and recovering of sight to the blind, to set at liberty those who are oppressed, and to announce that the time had come when you would save your people. He healed the sick, fed the hungry, and ate with sinners.

By the baptism of his suffering, death, and resurrection, you gave birth to your Church, delivered us from slavery to sin and death, and made with us a new covenant by water and the Spirit. When the Lord Jesus ascended, he promised to be with us always, in the power of your Word and Holy Spirit.

On the night in which he gave himself up for us he took bread, gave thanks to you, broke the bread, gave it to his disciples, and said: "Take, eat; this is my body which is given for you. Do this in remembrance of me."

When the supper was over he took the cup, gave thanks to you, gave it to his disciples, and said: "Drink from this, all of you; this is my blood of the new covenant, poured out for you and for many for the forgiveness of sins. Do this, as often as you drink it, in remembrance of me."

And so, in remembrance of these your mighty acts in Jesus Christ, we offer ourselves in praise and thanksgiving as a holy and living sacrifice, in union with Christ's offering for us, as we proclaim the mystery of faith.

b. Memorial Acclamation (Sung or read by the people.)

CHRIST HAS DIED, CHRIST HAS RIS - EN. CHRIST WILL COME A - GAIN.

Pour out your Holy Spirit on us, gathered here, and on these gifts of bread and wine. Make them be for us the body and blood of Christ, that we may be for the world the body of Christ, redeemed by his blood.

By your Spirit make us one with Christ, one with each other, and one in ministry to all the world, until Christ comes in final victory and we feast at his heavenly banquet.

Through your Son Jesus Christ, with the Holy Spirit in your holy Church, all honor and glory is yours, almighty Father, now and forever.

c. Great Amen (Sung or read by the people.)

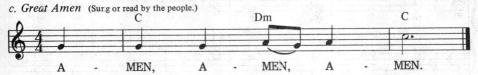

Ard now, with the confidence of children of God, let us pray (said or sung):

OUR FATHER IN HEAVEN, HALLOWED BY YOUR NAME,
YOUR KINGDOM COME, YOUR WILL BE DONE,
ON EARTH AS IN HEAVEN.
GIVE US TODAY OUR DAILY BREAD.
FORGIVE US OUR SINS
AS WE FORGIVE THOSE WHO SIN AGAINST US.
SAVE US FROM THE TIME OF TRIAL AND DELIVER US FROM EVIL.
FOR THE KINGDOM, THE POWER, AND THE GLORY
ARE YOURS NOW AND FOR EVER. AMEN.

BREAKING THE BREAD

(The minister breaks the bread in silence, or while saying:)

Because there is one loaf, we, who are many, are one body, for we all partake of the one loaf. The bread which we break is a sharing in the body of Christ.

(The minister lifts the cup in silence, or while saying:)

The cup over which we give thanks is a sharing in the blood of Christ.

GIVING THE BREAD AND CUP

(The bread and wine are given to the people, with these or other words being exchanged:)

The body of Christ, given for you. AMEN.

The blood of Christ, given for you. AMEN.

(There may be singing or silence during the giving of bread and cup. When all have received, the Lord's table is put in order.)

Eternal God, we give you thanks for this holy mystery in which you have given yourself to us. Grant that we may go into the world in the strength of your Spirit, to give ourselves for others. In the name of Jesus Christ our Lord. AMEN.

SENDING FORTH

[HYMN OR SONG]

DISMISSAL WITH BLESSING

Go forth in peace.
The grace of the Lord Jesus Christ, and the love of God, and the communion of the Holy Spirit be with you all. AMEN.

GOING FORTH

(An instrumental postlude, spontaneous singing, or silence may follow, as appropriate.)

118a • Sanctus and Benedictus *(Accompaniment)*

Ho - ly, ho - ly, ho - ly Lord, God of pow - er and might,

heav - en and earth are full of your glo - ry. Ho - san - na in the

high - est. Bless - ed is he who comes in the name of the Lord. Ho -

ICET   Elise S. Eslinger

Music ©1985 by The Upper Room. Text is from *Prayers We Have in Common,* 2nd revised ed., 1975. Used by permission of ICET.

san - na in the high - est.

118b • Memorial Acclamation

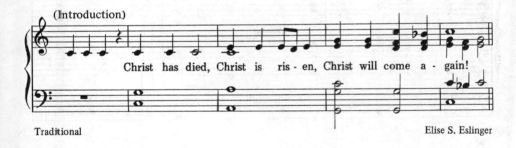

(Introduction)

Christ has died, Christ is ris - en, Christ will come a - gain!

Traditional   Elise S. Eslinger

118c • Great Amen

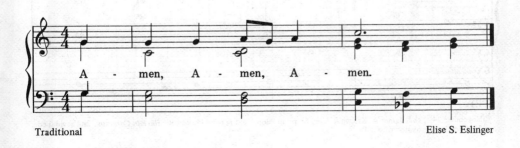

A - men, A - men, A - men.

Traditional   Elise S. Eslinger

119 • Service Music—Alternate I

119a • Sanctus and Benedictus

Ho - ly, ho - ly, ho - ly Lord, God of power and might,

heav'n and earth are full of your glo - ry. Ho - san - na in the

high - est. Bless - ed is he who comes in the name of the

Lord. Ho - san - na in the high - est.

119b • Memorial Acclamation

Christ has died. Christ is ris - en. Christ will come a - gain.

Traditional   James A. Kriewald

119c • Great Amen

A - men, A - men.
Al - le - lu - ia, Al - le - lu - ia.
A - men, A - men.

Traditional   James A. Kriewald

120 • Service Music—Alternate II

120a • Sanctus and Benedictus

Ho - ly, ho - ly, ho - ly Lord, God of power and might, heaven and earth are full of your glo - ry. Ho - san - na in the high - est. Bless - ed is he who comes in the name of the

ICET

John S. Rice

Music written 1981, John S. Rice. Used by permission. Text is from *Prayer: We Have in Common*, 2nd revised ed., 1975. Used by permission.

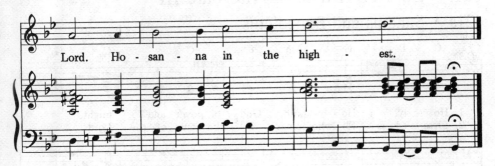

Lord. Ho - san - na in the high - est.

120b • Memorial Acclamation

Christ has died, Christ is ris - en, Christ will come a - gain.

Traditional

John S. Rice

120c • Great Amen

A - men. A - men.

A men.

Traditional

John S. Rice

121a • Sanctus and Benedictus

1. Ho - ly, Ho - ly Lord, God of pow'r and might,
2. Bless - ed is He who comes in the name of the Lord,

Heav - en and earth are full, full of your glo - ry, Ho -
Bless - ed is He who comes, comes in the name of the Lord, Ho -

san - na in the high - est.
san - na in the high - est. est.

DESCANT

Ho - ly, Ho - ly, Al - le - lu - ia, Ho - ly, Ho - ly,

Al - le - lu - ia, Ho - san - na in the high - est.

ICET
Adapt. Jim Strathdee

Jim Strathdee

121b • Memorial Acclamation

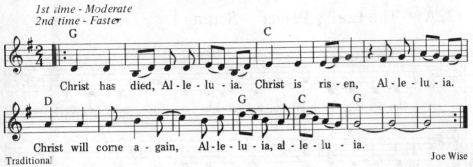

1st time - Moderate
2nd time - Faster

Christ has died, Al-le-lu-ia. Christ is ris-en, Al-le-lu-ia.
Christ will come a-gain, Al-le-lu-ia, al-le-lu-ia.

Traditional

Joe Wise

Optional Accompaniment:

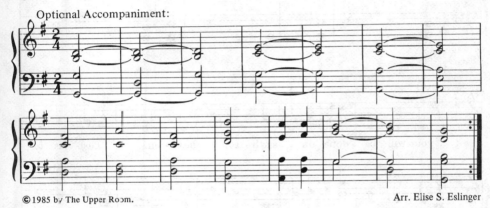

Arr. Elise S. Eslinger

121c • Great Amen

A - men, A - men,
A - men, Oh, Lawd-y! A - men, Have mer-cy!

A - men, A - men, A - men.   men.
A - men, A - men, A - men. Sing it o-ver now, men.

Traditional

Traditional
Harm. J. Jefferson Cleveland
and Verolga Nix

122 • The Lord's Prayer *(Musical Settings)*

122A • The Lord's Prayer—Setting I

Matthew 6:9-13
ICET

John Erickson

as we for-give those who sin a-gainst us.

Save us from the time of tri-al and de-liv-er us

from e-vil. For the king-dom, the pow-er, and the glo-ry

are yours now and for ev-er. A-men.

122B • The Lord's Prayer—Setting II

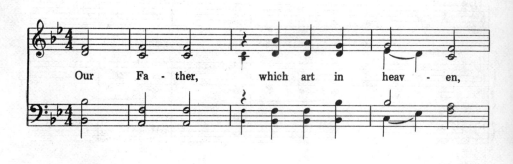

Our Fa - ther, which art in heav - en,

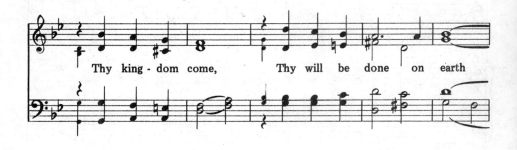

hal - low - ed be Thy name.

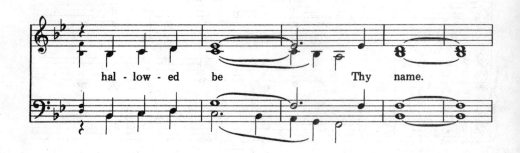

Thy king - dom come, Thy will be done on earth

as it is in heav - en.

Matthew 6:9-13, adapted

Albert Hay Malotte

122C • The Lord's Prayer—Setting III

Matthew 6:9-13
Adapt. Jim Strathdee

Source Unknown
Arr. Al Oppenheimer
Acc. Jim Strathdee

122D • The Lord's Prayer—Setting IV

1. Our Fa-ther, which art in heav-en,
2. Done on earth as it is in heav-en,
3. And for-give all our debts,
4. Lead us not in-to temp-ta-tion,
5. Thine is the king-dom, pow-er, and glo-ry,
6. A - men, a - men, a - men,

Hal-low-ed-a be Thy name.

Thy king-dom come, Thy will be done,
Give us this day our dai - ly bread,
As we for-give our debt - ors,
But de - liv - er us from e - vil,
For - ev - er, and ev - er,
A - men, a - men, a - men, a - men.

Hal-low-ed-a be Thy name.

*Guitar chords in D Major. Do not play guitar chords with piano accompaniment.

Matthew 6:9-13
Adapt. J. Jefferson Cleveland and Verolga Nix

West Indian Folk Tune
Arr. J. Jefferson Cleveland
and Verolga Nix

122E • The Lord's Prayer—Setting V

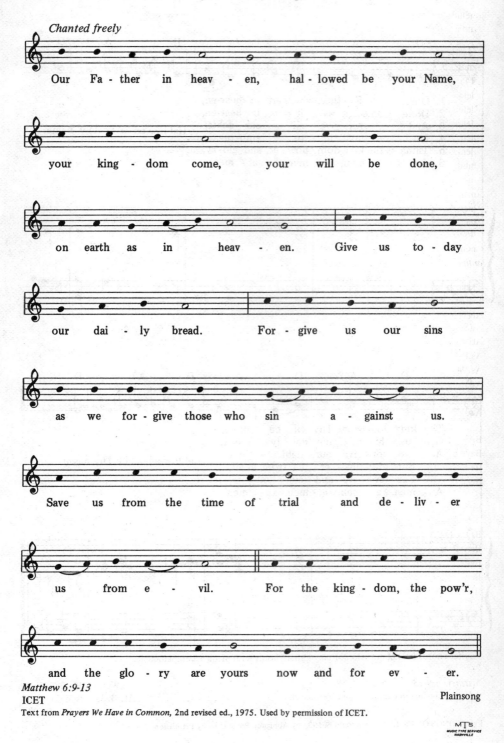

Chanted freely

Our Fa - ther in heav - en, hal - lowed be your Name,

your king - dom come, your will be done,

on earth as in heav - en. Give us to - day

our dai - ly bread. For - give us our sins

as we for - give those who sin a - gainst us.

Save us from the time of trial and de - liv - er

us from e - vil. For the king - dom, the pow'r,

and the glo - ry are yours now and for ev - er.

Matthew 6:9-13
ICET

Plainsong

Text from *Prayers We Have in Common,* 2nd revised ed., 1975. Used by permission of ICET.

123 • GENERAL INDEX
(Alphabetical)

Includes titles and first line alternate titles of musical selections; authors, composers, sources, translators and arrangers; and useful categories.

African Melody **36, 53**
Agnus Dei **70**
All Praise to You **21C**
Alleluia (Eight-fold) **71**
Alleluia (My Word) **43**
Alleluia, Sing for Joy **74**
Allen, Art **62**
Allen, Patricia **42**
Ambrose of Milan **21A**
Amen, The Great **118c, 119c, 120c, 121c**
Amen (Traditional) **121c**
Amen, Praise the Father **83**
American Folk Tune **56**
    (*See also* Early American Tunes)
Anonymous **71, 73, 74, 77, 105**
Antiphoner 1681 **18, 18A**

ANTIPHONAL PSALMS **94, 105, 110**

ANTIPHONS, PSALM
    (See Section IV) **87-111**
Arise, Your Light Has Come **19**
As Pilgrims on Our Way **21E**
As We Gather **41**
Atkinson, Frederick C. **10**
Avery, Richard and Donald Marsh **58**
Awake, Awake to Love and Work **20**

BAPTISM **23B**
Bayly, Albert F. **23**
Be Present at Our Table, Lord **102A**
Beethoven, Ludwig von **3**

BENEDICTIONS **78, 84, 85, 86**
    (*See also* Nunc Dimittis)
Benedictus **113, 113A, 113B, 113C**
Benedictus, Sanctus and **118a, 119a, 120a, 121a**
Berthier, Jacques **67, 68, 82**
Bewes, Richard **36**
BIBLICAL TEXTS
    Colossians 3:16 **88**
    Corinthians I-13 **56**
    Deuteronomy 32 11 **13**
    Isaiah 40:31 **65**
    Isaiah 43, sel. **42**
    Isaiah 55:12 **84**
    Isaiah 61:1 **47**
    Jeremiah 29:11-14; 31:3, 13 **44**
    John 13:3-5 **53**
    John 14:27 **85**

Luke 1:46-55 **115 115A, 115B**
Luke 1:68-79 **113 113A, 113B**
Luke 1:78-79 **113C**
Luke 2:29-32 **117, 117A, 117B, 117C**
Luke 24:13-35 **34**
Matthew 6:9-13 (The Lord's Prayer) **112, 114, 116, 118, 122A-E**
Matthew 6:33, 7:7 **64, 66**
Matthew 11:29 **64**
Philippians 2:10, 1 **73**
Psalms (see PSALMS)
Romans 14:8-9 **57**
Bless the Lord **104-I**
Bless'd Be the God of Israel **113B**
Blessed Be the God of Israel **113A**
Bortniansky, Dimitri S. **26**
Bourgeois, Louis **102**
Brother, Let Me Be Your Servant **54**

Cameron, Catherine **5A**
Can We, as Pilgrims **21E**
CANTICLES, BIBLICAL
    Mary **115, 115A, 115B**
    Simeon **117, 117A, 117B, 117C**
    Zachary **113, 113A, 113B, 113C**
        (*See also* Section V, Introduction)
Care the Eagle Gives Her Young, The **13**
Carter, Sydney **50**
Chamberlain, Gary **91, 92, 98, 99, 104, 106, 107, 109, 110**
CHANT (*See* OSTINATO AND CHANT)
Christ Has Died **113b, 119b, 120b, 121b**
Christ Is the Truth, the Way **11**
Church's One Foundation, The **14**
Clark, Jodi **42**
Cleveland, J. Jefferson **75, 111, 122D**
Coffman, Mary Ruth **90**
Colvin, Tom **53**
Come, Let Us Sing **99**
Come, My Way, My Truth, My Life **35**
Come to Me **64**
Come, We That Love the Lord **12**
COMMUNION (*See* HOLY COMMUNION)
Cothran, Jeff **38**
Create in Me a Clean Heart **94**
(*See also* **95**)
Create Us New **81**
Creating God, Your Fingers Trace **1A**
Creator God, Creating Still **22A**

123A • AN INDEX OF TUNE NAMES